How She Does It

ALSO BY MARGARET HEFFERNAN

The Naked Truth

How She Does It

HOW WOMEN ENTREPRENEURS ARE
CHANGING THE RULES OF BUSINESS SUCCESS

Margaret Heffernan

VIKING

VIKING
Published by the Penguin Group
Penguin Group (USA) Inc., 375 Hudson Street,
New York, New York 10014, U.S.A.
Penguin Group (Canada), 90 Eglinton Avenue East, Suite 700,
Toronto, Ontario, Canada M4P 2Y3 (a division of Pearson Penguin Canada Inc.)
Penguin Books Ltd, 80 Strand, London WC2R 0RL, England
Penguin Ireland, 25 St. Stephen's Green, Dublin 2, Ireland
(a division of Penguin Books Ltd)
Penguin Books Australia Ltd, 250 Camberwell Road, Camberwell,
Victoria 3124, Australia
(a division of Pearson Australia Group Pty Ltd)
Penguin Books India Pvt Ltd, 11 Community Centre, Panchsheel Park,
New Delhi – 110 017, India
Penguin Group (NZ), Cnr Airborne and Rosedale Roads, Albany,
Auckland 1310, New Zealand
(a division of Pearson New Zealand Ltd)
Penguin Books (South Africa) (Pty) Ltd, 24 Sturdee Avenue,
Rosebank, Johannesburg 2196, South Africa

Penguin Books Ltd, Registered Offices:
80 Strand, London WC2R 0RL, England

First published in 2007 by Viking Penguin,
a member of Penguin Group (USA) Inc.

10 9 8 7 6 5 4 3 2 1

Copyright © Margaret Heffernan, 2007
All rights reserved

ISBN: 978-0-670-03823-7

Printed in the United States of America
Set in Bembo with Gill Sans
Designed by Daniel Lagin

For Felix and Leonora

Contents

Contents

PART 3
The Only Failure Is Not to Try

Introduction

This is a book of stories.

But it starts with numbers.

Forty percent of all privately held U.S. firms are owned or controlled by women. This represents 10.4 million firms.

Between 1997 and 2004, privately held, women-owned businesses grew at twice the rate of all other U.S. firms.

Women's companies are creating jobs at twice the rate of all firms and are now responsible for more payroll than all the Fortune 500 companies combined.

Women's companies are growing profits faster than all firms.

Women's companies are more likely than others to stay in business, while companies owned by women of color are four times as likely as others to stay in business.

Every day in America, 420 new women-owned businesses are formed.

These are phenomenal numbers. They defy logic. The business world isn't a level playing field, and women receive far less in the way of institutional investment and Small Business Administration (SBA) loans than other businesses. And they receive only

5 percent of all venture capital.[1] So not only are women doing really well, but their businesses are thriving when the playing field is tilted against them. That makes these numbers all the more incredible.

Naysayers, skeptics, and curmudgeons will try to tell you that this isn't really meaningful. After all, they'll say, only 4 percent of women-owned businesses have revenues over a million dollars. True, but only 6 percent of *all* businesses have revenues over a million dollars. Ninety-nine percent of America's businesses are small companies, and they provide more than half the jobs. Small is not trivial. Moreover, women's companies with revenues over a million dollars and women's companies with more than a hundred employees are growing at twice the rate of all companies. There are therefore more of those bigger women-owned companies every year.

But, they'll go on, women's businesses aren't really where the action is. They're all cookie companies, bed-and-breakfasts, and funky little boutiques. Wrong, wrong, wrong. The biggest growth sectors for women's businesses are: wholesale trade, health care services, arts, entertainment and recreation, and professional, scientific, and technical services. In the economy overall, the highest growth isn't in the tech sector but in the services sector—right where the women are.

But, the pessimists persist, women aren't really risk takers. This argument collapses in the face of the evidence that women take on more personal debt to fund their businesses than men do, and they're generally more willing than men to go out on a limb. Cautious they may be, but risk-averse they certainly are not.

Defeated by the facts, curmudgeons will point to Martha Stewart with a flourish. There—doesn't she prove that women just can't cut it? But hers is one story out of ten million. The trend says so much more than the headline, and that trend has real momentum. The more women-owned businesses succeed, the more respect and funding they are starting to get. The more funding they get, the more they can succeed.

That their companies are doing so well says a great deal about female strengths and talents. As long as women continue to slug it out in traditional companies that were built by men for men, much of their energy will go into fitting into those cultures. It is a big drain on resources. But once a woman runs her own company, that drain evaporates. These phenomenal numbers show just how effective women can be when they work on their own terms. They also demonstrate just how much talent those traditional corporations lose when their women give up on them.

The growth and success of women-owned businesses is one of the most profound changes taking place in the business world today. It challenges us to ask: Why? What do women do to make their businesses so successful? With so many companies doing so well, how can you explain that success? And what lessons can we all learn from them?

Those are the questions that this book seeks to answer. When I set out to study a representative group of companies, my sample needed to include both new and established companies. It needed to represent all the major industrial sectors and to have a broad geographic spread. I wanted it to be broadly reflective of the modern economy. I didn't go looking for exemplary companies, and I didn't start with any predefined criteria except that each company had to be majority owned or controlled by a woman. Taking these companies as a whole, I then asked myself what meaningful characteristics they had in common. I didn't embark on this quest as an academic but as someone who has run five businesses herself. Having stood in a CEO's shoes, I have some insight into what is required to build a business from scratch: the nightmares, sleeplessness, and worry that some small misstep will prove to have enormous unforeseen consequences.

Talking to hundreds of women business owners, I came to see a number of patterns, common themes that persisted regardless of industry, company size, or age. The differences between the companies are huge. Some are run by highly trained intellects, some by high school dropouts. Some are family businesses; others will never be. But far more striking than the differences were the similarities.

Generalizations about female ways of working or feminine talents make every woman queasy. For centuries we have seen how any acknowledgment of difference can pave the way to stereotyping, discrimination, and inequality. This has often made us defensive about our gifts and hesitant to draw attention to them. Moreover, we all know that there is no single, uniform, female way of doing anything. We have seen many men work in "female" ways just as we have seen a lot of women work like guys.

But as I traveled from company to company, regardless of size or sector, it became impossible not to notice that these women had a way of working and, more important, a way of being that came to be recognizable and even predictable. After a while I knew what I might find, and I just kept on finding it.

Some of the conclusions in this book have made me very uncomfortable, but I couldn't avoid them. Yes, women do work differently from men. Yes, they are really good at what they do. And, yes, the way they run their companies goes some significant way to explaining the fantastic explosion of women-owned busi-

nesses. It is enlightening. It is inspiring. It challenges many assumptions about what matters when you're running a company.
And if we let it, it would teach us all—men *and* women—a great
deal about how to build a new business order that we can be
proud of.

Part I

Fire in the Belly, Skin in the Game

1. The Need to Achieve

In the spring of 2000, I was running a high-tech company in Boston. It was backed by CMGi, a publicly traded company that invested in Internet start-ups. The Internet bubble did nothing to make running a high-growth business easy, and CMGi, run by David Wetherell, had a strikingly toxic culture. I was the only female CEO among forty and the only one with a working spouse. This wasn't the first business I had run, but it was certainly the most grueling.

One afternoon when flying from San Francisco to Los Angeles, I ran into David Bohnett, founder and CEO of GeoCities, one of the jewels in CMGi's crown. The company had gone public at $3 billion and had been bought by Yahoo! David was one of the few CEOs whom I could regard as a soul mate. I was female in a macho world; he was gay. We were destined to be friends.

Sitting together that afternoon, David asked me a great question: "Why do you do it? Why are you so prepared to go balls to the wall with Wetherell? What drives you?" Many guys had left. I had outlasted a whole series of tough, macho CEOs, some of whom had stayed less than a year. I had to think hard to answer David's question, and in the end my answer surprised me.

"It's the people. I've hired a lot of really great people—Russians, Chinese, gay women, gay men, single parents—all brilliantly talented. I can't let them down. I have to keep going."

I had always thought that the benefit of becoming an entrepreneur would be working for myself and having my employees work for me. It turned out to be the other way around.

Women are starting their own businesses at such a phenomenal rate that it is natural to wonder why. When starting a new business is so hard and so risky, what makes it appealing to increasing waves of women?

The study of entrepreneurial motivation is fraught with inconclusions. Entrepreneurs are clearly different from corporate executives—but quite how and why, no one is sure. Studies do show that for neither men nor women is money the prime driver. Instead, entrepreneurs seek adventure; they want to learn more and want to stretch themselves. Many had entrepreneurial parents. But the fact that more women than ever—420 a day—are starting new businesses suggests that something extra is driving them. Some of this is a collision of social and economic trends. More and more women are well educated.[1] There is a larger pool of women with high-level experience of traditional businesses.[2] There is a rise in entrepreneurship throughout the world's economy.[3] Much of this is undoubtedly fueled by the development of new technologies that make it cheaper and easier than ever to set up in business for yourself.

But the single reason most often cited by women to explain why they go into business for themselves is simple: they want independence.[4] They seek control of their own destiny. They don't want to be passive victims of corporations and strategies and men who don't value them.

"I quit over dinner. I just got to the boiling point, and I quit. Walked out of the restaurant, went back to my hotel room, called my husband, and said I'd quit. I said, 'Everyone else has his or her own business. Why not me?' So we started in March 1999."

Cecilia McCloy is a geologist. She worked for SAIC, a research and engineering firm, for twelve years, which by any measure would make her a loyal employee. But she reached boiling point, she said, because it got so hard to have any influence. Reorganization followed reorganization until her ability to have any impact on the people or the company felt negligible. It hadn't helped that as the only female vice president she was always being asked by other women to lend support to their sexual harassment suits. The women expected her to advance their cause while the men repeatedly ignored her. The overriding issue was that, despite her rank, men kept making decisions about her and about her people without consulting her.

Cecilia felt—as so many women feel in corporate America—invisible. Every woman can tell you stories of not being heard in meetings, of work not being rewarded, of promotions that somehow just don't happen. These careers follow a predictable trajectory. At the outset of her career, a young woman, pretty and eager to please, is trivialized, appreciated for her charm but little else. As she gains in competence and confidence, she becomes invisible. Struggling to assert herself, she is castigated for being too aggressive, a bitch. If she keeps trying, she may eventually assimilate and be seen as a guy, but then she is shunned by women for having sold out.[5]

These stereotypes dog women's careers and leave them feeling either depressed or frustrated. Why, they wonder, can't I be valued for who and what I am? Why must I constantly struggle to fit into a business world that insists on seeing my strengths as weaknesses? That sees my ability to bear children as some unmentionable threat? That sees my emotions and intuition and empathy as trivial? Where can I go to tap the ability and creativity that I know I have?

"I was working at Unisys, and they'd just had their merger. We had had twenty-three org charts in thirty days," recalled Lurita Doan. "I didn't know who I was working for, and with each chart I fell lower and lower until my UNIX group wasn't even on the chart. We were just one little circle on the side. I didn't know what that meant, but I knew it was bad!

"I had an idea of how to become a program manager and went to my boss and told him. I'd been up all night working on the business plan for it. I explained that at our customer sites there was always stuff left undone. They needed custom work, and it seemed logical to me that we should do that work. So I said I'd do it. And my boss just said, 'That's the stupidest thing in the world. No one will pay for that.'

"I went home, and I was so upset. My husband said, 'Why don't you just quit? You are so bossy and always know what's right. Why not just do it?' So I did! Best thing I ever did because I do like to have my own way and I am usually right."

For centuries women have known what it is to be powerless, to be dependent, but now they have the skills and, increasingly, the confidence to stand up for themselves. The independence they seek is not just professional. Women in high-growth businesses may not put money at the top of their list of motivators, but they do put it second. This is not about fast cars and big houses. For women, financial independence is about not being held hostage to a marriage or a job that no longer satisfies. It is about having choices.

What is so interesting is that women are not leaving traditional careers just to get out. Lurita Doan wasn't running away, and Cecilia McCloy didn't retire to the kitchen to bake cookies. Nor do they storm out in a huff and regret it the next day. These women are moving from positions where they are undervalued, underestimated, and unsatisfied to something far more demanding. It is an existential flight to a place where who and what they are, how they like to work, and the things they care about are not just tolerated but are given a dynamic and central role. Disappointed by the rigid, narrow choices that so many careers appear to offer, women strike out on their own to redefine what is possible.

That women are willing to embrace huge risks in their search for self-determination says everything about how urgent this quest is. It is no small thing to leave a big successful career like SAIC, as Cecilia McCloy did; or to leave Wall Street, as Pat Loret de Mola did; or to leave BP, as did Carol Latham, a divorced mother of three college-bound children. "You put your life on the table," said Carol. "But I had to do it. I knew I could do it. I knew I could bring a product to market." All these women—and there are millions like them—were driven to look for a place where they could prove themselves on their own terms. There is some evidence that women are willing to take bigger risks with their careers than men. This is not because they are stupid; it is because they're desperate.[6] So often they can see no other way to find work, and a way of working, that suits them. Why do they embrace the risk? Because they must.

"When my company was taken over," said Joni Walton, CEO of Danlee Medical Supplies, "I asked what they would do to my division, and they said, 'Dissolve it.' This was a division I'd started by myself inside the company, and without even talking to me about it, they were going to shut it down!

"I stood up—I was so angry—and I said, 'You have to let me buy it.' They said, 'Are you serious? Okay, maybe we can do a deal.' I was shocked. I was just being a big mouth! I went home to my husband and told him what had happened, and all he said was 'We have only $500 in the bank.' I also had a four-year-old son."

Joni Walton had no experience running a business. She had nothing: no degree, no assets, no collateral. She just had a burning desire to keep her achievement from being obliterated. When no bank would help her, Joni found a backer, a former boss, who lent her $25,000. That eventually ballooned to $100,000. The business *had* to be successful; there was no other conceivable way that she could repay what she owed. There could be no turning back.

It is an irony that in their demand for independence, both financial and personal, women feel compelled to take on such huge exposure. Once again it shows just how urgent they feel their quest to be. Women are more likely to fund their companies with personal debt.[7] Some of this is because it is harder for them to obtain venture capital or commercial loans, but some of it is because they are just so determined to succeed.

"I was a divorced single woman with three kids who were heading for college," Carol Latham recalled. "I was absolutely on my own, and I didn't come from money. No one in our family had money. My mother loaned me $10,000, and you know what parents are like: I'd rather have died than not repay that money. But apart from that, I just had nothing. That's my definition of an entrepreneur. The five *no*s: no product, no customers, no plant, no money, no employees. And maybe a sixth no: no safety net."

Carol believed she had found a way to reduce the heat generated by computers. She had no safety net; what she had was fire in her belly. Like thousands of her peers, she was driven to prove herself. For Carol, what mattered most was her belief in her product. But equally important to her and to most women is a passion for the *way* that business gets done. Having been marginalized, trivialized, berated, and frustrated, women set out with not just one tough goal but two: to prove that they can succeed and to work in their own way.

"The year I turned thirty," said Mona Eliassen, "I got so bored. The owners taught me nothing, so I gave two weeks' notice and quit. Partly, I got sick and thought maybe I hated my job. I'm feisty. I'm used to being on my own and to not having much. I wanted to see if I could work on my own terms in my own way."

At its simplest, "working in my own way" means "determining my own hours." Fifty-nine percent of women say they have no flexibility about the start and end of their day.[8] They are constantly being told, explicitly or implicitly, that they must choose either career or family. But they reject that polarization, insisting that it is possible to have both. For that reason their ambitions are routinely trivialized. Women, the received wisdom goes, just run lifestyle businesses that they can balance with their child care obligations. The implication is that they aren't very serious. This is a gross insult to every entrepreneur I know. There is nothing harder or more demanding than running your own company. The fact that it is flexible, that you can call the shots, does nothing to make it easy. Doris Christopher started The Pampered Chef because all the available jobs made it impossible for her to give her family the time and attention she wanted to give them. The fact that she stuck to her guns and went on to found a huge successful business says more about the paucity of choices available to her than about her galvanic energy or commitment.

When you start your own business, you can work your own way. You are the boss. And so business becomes a way of proving that the old, stale, male ways of working are not exclusive avenues to success. We don't have to choose between work and family. We don't have to measure employees' value by how many evenings and weekends they're prepared to sacrifice. We don't have to do business via shoot-outs and bake-offs. Macho work environments, rigid career patterns, turf wars, and internal competition—these are not women's ways of working. They are profoundly alienating, and while not all women start their business with a mission to overturn age-old business paradigms, many do.

"I've always had such personal beliefs about the way that business *should* be done," said Geraldine Laybourne, CEO of the cable network Oxygen. "I feel that I have a lot to prove. I like challenging the muscle man theory of doing business. What is it they're saying—nice is the new mean?"

Geraldine has worked in some of the biggest, most volatile, and competitive media companies in the world, and she has succeeded there. She has proved she can work that way. What she wants to prove now is that you don't have to.

Women starting new businesses have something to prove. They may need to prove to themselves that the companies that undervalued them in the past were wrong. They may need to prove their idea is right or that they really can repay a personal loan. They may need to prove that their values, their instincts, and their natural ways of working are just as good and just as effective as the "muscle man" styles they've grown up with. It may be all those things.[9] Such women have a lot of psychic skin in the game. In this respect, women entrepreneurs remind me of a wave of immigrants: driven out of a land they found hostile, taking big risks in their determination to create a New World where they can succeed on their own terms. America was built by such pioneers and, today, its economy continues to be enriched by the fresh thinking of women who don't accept defeat.

But then, once they get started, and experience even a small degree of success, women's motivation undergoes a subtle but profound shift. Where once they had something to prove to themselves, now they have something they want to prove for others. Liberated to work in their own way, women discover the power that comes from liberating others.

"I realize I'm driven," confesses Brenda Rivers, the founder and CEO of Andavo Travel, a $100 million business. "The drive is about independence and money, but the money is about creating a company that is great for employees who can grow and have the freedom to express themselves. It is about so much more than profit. It's about making a better home for the employees. Work may be hard, boring, frustrating, but they *know* they're valued. And I feel a real duty to give back however I can. One way I can give back is by being very successful. I am very, very passionate about people."

As they become more successful by working in their own way and on their own terms, women develop a sense of their own power and become tremendously motivated by what that power can do for other people. Some women may have known this at the outset, but they all seem to learn that there is an inalienable connection between nurturing their dream company and nurturing their people. This phenomenon plays to the female strengths that past employers may have dismissed as weakness.

"My characters, I'm really proud of them. They have a schedule for kitchen duties. Some of them—heck, I potty-trained the guys: Put the seat down, don't pee with it down. John kept leaving his glasses at his girlfriend's, so I got him Lasik surgery so he wouldn't have to worry about it. Willy had no education or training at all. We trained him, and we weren't sure he'd make it—and now he is incredible. We give him big powerful things to do, and he does them. It changed his whole life. It's growth for them."

This isn't necessarily what you'd expect to hear from the CEO of an innovative high-tech company, but that's what Nadine Lange is. No one would describe her as sentimental or a soft touch. She is a smart, hard-charging boss with high expectations of herself and others. She is also very driven to look after her people—or, as she calls them, her characters.

"Kaki's the one I've known longest. She's in sales. For a long time she was making so much money at SAP that I didn't feel in a position to hire her. She is her family's breadwinner—how could I? Now that she's here and works so hard, I have to make it work—because look at what I've asked her to leave behind! I can't let her down now."

Nadine's company has grown by at least 40 percent every year for the last three years. She may be looking after her "characters," but far from interfering with her business, it is her devotion to them that is building her company. Time and again when I asked women what kept them going, not just through the start-up phase but long after the company had proved itself, they said the same thing: looking after the people.

I didn't go out of my way to find nurturing, passionate business owners. I just kept running into them—not just in the so-called caring professions but in every kind of business: manufacturing, agriculture, high-tech, food, electronics, financial services. Every woman I spoke to may have had a slightly different reason for starting her business: to get out of corporate America, to support herself through a divorce, to pursue an idea no one appreciated. These were canny, hardheaded, hardworking businesswomen; they weren't Mother Theresa-like altruists. But what motivated them after they had started was strikingly uniform: They were all driven to succeed *for* their workforce. They may have started for themselves, but they kept going for others.

This has profound implications for the businesses women run and the way they run them. The bond between looking after the business and looking after the people is not rhetoric, and nurturing isn't weakness; it is what explains their success. When you feel such passionate affinity with, and responsibility for, your employees, then you put values, ethics, and culture squarely at the center of every decision you make. Mistakes are less frightening, and seeking help is less intimidating. It makes you profoundly connected, courageous, and creative. And as motivation it provides inexhaustible staying power.

If that sounds a bit too much like social work, it is worth remembering that these companies are highly lucrative. Nadine Lange's Open Scan doubled its revenues this year. Carol Latham's Thermagon is famous for some of the highest margins in her industry. Joni Walton's medical supply business is regularly courted by suitors who can't quite see how she manages to be so much more profitable than her competitors. Women's businesses aren't just growing in number; they're growing their profits faster than other businesses. And in the obstacle race that is entrepreneurship, women are twice as likely to stay in business. Why shouldn't they? Their motivation is of the highest order.

Outside of professional sports, it is hard to imagine anything more grueling than starting and running your own business. It makes demands of every aspect of your intelligence, and it is unrelenting. As Doreen Marks of Otis Technology once remarked to me, "It doesn't really matter *which* eighty hours you work." The sense of responsibility—for employees, for suppliers, and for customers—never lets up, just as the demand to innovate, to cut costs, to boost margins, and to find new markets never stops. At the back of your mind is the failure rate: Almost all new businesses fail. The women business owners I've met do not derive their tremendous stamina from ego, from overweening self-confidence, or from the confidence of institutions. They get it from the employees and business partners they see themselves *serving*.

Over the last ten years I have met hundreds of fascinating women business owners, many of whom you will meet in this book. They aren't obviously exceptional people. Some graduated college, some did not; most do not have an MBA—but they all had something to prove and have proved it. They have all been devoted to their people and to their businesses. One woman particularly stands out because she was an early pioneer who started with so little. (Indeed, it strikes me that there is a piece of inverse logic that says the less you have, the more you do for others.)

Carol Latham started her business, Thermagon, with nothing. She was divorced and her kids told her she was crazy. She rented out her home and went to live in an apartment, funding her dream on the difference. After years in the wilderness, her ideas started to take off and the company began to grow. A lot of these things are pretty typical of many entrepreneurial ventures. But what Carol did as the company grew wasn't typical. Situated in inner-city Cleveland, she desperately needed people. So she took the ones she could find, mostly Hispanics, inexperienced and uneducated. She hired them, she gave them chances—and she gave them classes.

"We'd screen them to see if they'd fit, if they had the right attitude. We'd test people for basic math. Their English was not always very good, so I got the Cleveland school system to provide us with teachers and we taught them English, math, and computer skills—all on company time. We had a classroom right here in the factory! And lots of them did so well, they got lots of promotions. And then they'd recommend someone else. We ended up hiring lots of inner-city Latinos and Hispanics. The impact on peoples' lives has just been phenomenal."

I can't tell you what drove Carol more—her desire to prove herself or her desire to look after her employees. I don't think she could separate the two. In the course of building her company, Carol made many discoveries that were breakthroughs in thermal conductivity. But her biggest discovery of all was the power she gained when she gave free rein to her instinct for looking after people.

"It's a pretty neat thing. You can create value out of nothing! Nothing—that's what we started with. You create value out of nothing with people just by giving them a chance to prove themselves." That's what business is. That's how women do it—by giving themselves a chance first and then giving chances, help, and support to others. It is a very virtuous circle.

2. Zeitgeist

I n 1986, I bought my first computer. It was a big ugly thing, and it was fiercely difficult to use. You had to load each program as you needed it. Having no graphic interface, you had to remember command line instructions to get it to work. It wasn't a time saver. I guess I got it because computers were proliferating in business, and I hated not knowing what they did or how they worked. They were used mostly by accountants for spreadsheets and by secretaries for word processing. Executive men didn't use them because they wouldn't be caught dead typing. Few imagined that just ten years later executives, both male and female, would be carrying book-thin computers in their briefcases to and from work every day. But petite, blond Carol Latham did imagine it—and helped make it happen.

Carol has a BA in chemistry. "It sounds like an oxymoron," she said, "an arts degree in a science, but how else can you run a company?"

She spent several years working in plastics but then stayed home for seventeen years, raising her three children. Propelled back to work by divorce, she returned to Sohio, a materials company that was now focusing on heat-conducting ceramics. As

Intel prepared to launch its 386 chip, she knew that as computers got faster they would get hotter. "Miniaturization—which is what personal computers were all about—made things smaller, but it didn't make them any cooler. Heat is the limiting factor," she argued.

She argued further that ceramics wouldn't solve this problem but combining ceramics with plastics might. "I put forward a project saying we have to make a polymer semiconductor. That way you can mold it, form it. It won't be hard and brittle like ceramics. I started doing some experiments and got really unexpected results—higher than any literature suggested by a factor of ten!"

Her colleagues didn't want to know. "They showed very little interest. I wanted to be taken seriously. But there was a moat. A river. A mountain. I couldn't get anywhere. And I had this conviction, this absolute conviction that this was the way to solve a really big problem." That conviction led her to leave Sohio, start her own business, Thermagon, and start making polymer semiconductors. Then in 1995, as Intel prepared to launch its Pentium chip, heat *was* the limiting factor.

"Up until then," she recalled, "Intel didn't admit there was a problem with heat. But with the introduction of Pentium, they called me and asked if they could take some of our products and literature to their manufacturing partners in Asia. They wanted to know how their customers could get my materials. Did I have an agent in Taiwan? Of course I didn't, but I soon got one. I was very calm on the phone but very excited, too, of course."

Carol "had" zeitgeist—meaning she had captured, quite literally, the spirit of her time. She had a profound intuition about the market, where it was going and what it would need. And she trusted that instinct with her livelihood. In that, she is entirely consistent with most businesswomen, who take gut feeling very seriously.[1]

Being in tune with the zeitgeist is important in business because it allows you to capitalize on the spirit of the time before it is obvious to everyone. It has nothing to do with market research, which is always historical, recording what has already been felt or seen or needed—not what will be. When Carol talks about her frustrations with Sohio, who didn't want to know about her insights into polymers, she says that they had "tunnel vision." It's an apt phrase because capturing the zeitgeist is just the opposite of tunnel vision. It's about seeing widely, picking up lots of different signals, and making sense of them.

In studying emotional intelligence at work, Daniel Goleman analyzed research on hundreds of top executives at fifteen global companies. One cognitive ability distinguished star performers: pattern recognition. "It's the 'big picture' thinking that allows leaders to pick out the meaningful trends from the welter of information around them and to think far into the future."[2] In other words, it's sensing zeitgeist. It sounds a little fuzzy, but it's real and is a critical contributor to business success. It is also something that women are very good at.

The closest cousin of understanding zeitgeist is having empathy, being able to see things from the point of view of others and not yourself. Empathy isn't about being nice or agreeing with people. Empathy is about context, about observing more broadly than one's own perspective, and it is about picking up signals. Goleman calls empathy "social radar," but I would argue that it goes further than purely social relationships. What Carol Latham did was imagine herself in the position of a computer manufacturer. What would drive them? Miniaturization and processing speeds. What would inhibit them? Heat. What she did *not* do was think from Sohio's perspective: We make ceramics. What new kinds of ceramics can we invent to shove down people's throats? She thought from the manufacturer's perspective. She empathized with her customer.

Simon Baron-Cohen at Cambridge University claims (and wrote a book to substantiate the claim) that "the female brain is predominantly hard-wired for empathy." While I am not quite sure what "hard-wired" means or how you prove it, it is clear that hundreds of studies around the world have found that, on average, women are more empathetic than men.[3]

Baron-Cohen goes on to say that empathy involves inexactness (because we can only ever approximate others' feelings), attention to the bigger picture, context, and what he calls "no expectation of lawfulness," by which he means an acceptance that what was true yesterday may not be true today.[4] It is hard to imagine a better definition of the requirements for business leadership. You have to tolerate inexactness because you so frequently have to make decisions before all the data are in. You have to see the big picture because otherwise you can't discern patterns. You have to be able to see your business in context. And tolerance for change, for discontinuity, is the order of the day. Baron-Cohen's definition of empathy—that capability at which women excel and the capacity for which he says we are hard-wired—strikes me as being synonymous with fundamental business skills.

Not everyone believes this argument about hard-wired empathy. They prefer a historical explanation, arguing that women's empathy is the inheritance of years of powerlessness. People low in social power learn to read signals; they have to for their survival. Lacking institutional protection, their very lives or careers depend on being profoundly in tune with shifts in mood and attitude. As women we have been low in social power for a long time. The only way we have been able to achieve anything has often been by staying *off* the radar screen, which meant we needed to be aware of what was on it. We have learned to be vigilant, to pick up clues, to get the drift before it gets us.

Whichever explanation you prefer, women's empathy provides a wider world view, not only through their own eyes but through the eyes of others. It is a capacity that yields profound business advantage. It is not the tunnel vision of Carol Latham's colleagues but the peripheral vision that sees the importance of marginal events. Through history or chemistry we have become very good at picking up signals.

It helps that women are often to be found in places where those signals occur. We all know the figures: Women purchase 83 percent of all goods and services. We are responsible for 91 percent of home purchases, 88 percent of retail purchases, 89 percent of bank accounts, and more than 50 percent of credit card use, Internet use, and travel expenditure.[5] We send three times more gifts and greetings cards, write two to four times more personal letters, and make 10 to 20 percent more long distance calls.[6] This may occasionally make us the butt of jokes, but it also makes us very smart. We understand the market because we are *in* the market all the time, noticing new products, new trends, new failures, and new tastes. It is all part of the big picture that you have to see if you are going to recognize patterns. To be attuned to the zeitgeist is to be deeply and often chaotically informed.

What was the market research done by Doris Christopher when she launched The Pampered Chef? None. She noticed that many kitchen utensils were inadequate. She noticed that her friends admired the tools she used in her kitchen. She noticed that everyone was pressed for time and valued any implement that would save them time. That is capturing zeitgeist.

How did Eileen Fisher know that women were looking for simpler, more comfortable ways to dress, that they would need clothing that transitioned seamlessly from home to work and out to dinner? She wasn't even in the garment business when she started; she worked in restaurants. But she saw that women's lives were getting more and more complicated and that nothing in their wardrobe made their lives any easier. That is also tuning into the zeitgeist.

Because it is so intuitive, so inexact, and so invisible, trying to identify the zeitgeist can provoke opposition. No one at Sohio agreed with Carol Latham that only by combining ceramics with plastics could you beat the heat problem. No one in the U.S. government could see the connections that Kimberly Bunting saw, either.

"I spent years," she recalled, "working in the field of government training. I could see that businesses badly needed to hire well-trained people—the companies I represented hired more than forty thousand people a year! At the same time I could see that the government was spending plenty to train people—more than $10 billion a year! But no one could see that you could build a program that would bring those needs *together* without sacrificing one for the other. After fifteen years of trying to persuade government programs to redesign themselves, I determined that it would be easier to build it myself and sell it to them."

Kimberly's company, Business Access, is a multimillion-dollar business, but when she started, no one even saw that market. Market research could have told her nothing. Her sense of zeitgeist, her awareness that technology could bring together two separate constituents in a cost-effective way, told her everything she needed to know.

In the United Kingdom, Penny Streeter was quick to notice

a changing market. What I call zeitgeist she calls a fluke. "By a sheer fluke we stumbled upon the health care market. I noticed that there were a lot of new, swish nursing homes opening up, and I thought: That's great for the residents, but they must be impossible to staff. So our business was supplying staff to places that found it hard to get people."

Penny noticed this just as the market in private nursing homes was about to take off, but she did more than catch the wave. She thought long and hard about the challenges these kinds of businesses must face.

"Lots of these places needed people on very short notice. Our competition just diverted them to mobile phones, so they'd get someone who was cooking dinner or juggling a baby. I realized that the care business is a twenty-four-hour business and that if we were giving a good service, we had to be twenty-four hours, too." She called her business, aptly, Ambition 24Hours.

Her ability to empathize took her even further: "We supply staff to what I think of as the most vulnerable sector of society. Foremost in my mind is the fact that if I fell over and went to the hospital, what kind of person would I want to look after me? I realized that I'd need a very high level of trust, so we have always carried out much deeper checks into our people than the law required. At one point we scrutinized people so intensely that it was almost impossible to get through our process! But it meant we could attract senior medical and professional staff that would not normally dream of working with an agency."

Penny's entire business vision is driven by a sense of where the market is going and an ability to empathize with what it will need. Her biggest challenge now is not understanding the market but keeping up with it. Her first six years saw an overall growth rate of 257 percent, and last year alone it was 131 percent. Being in tune with the times has its rewards and its challenges.

Karen Caplan's business depends on catching the zeitgeist. "Frieda's made its name with new product introductions. We were the people who introduced the kiwi fruit into the United States. We never said no when people brought us mangoes or alfalfa sprouts. And these things were not 'in' at the time."

As a food distributor, Frieda's stands or falls by finding new food varieties and bringing them to market. Being in tune with that market is fundamental to staying in business.

"We put ourselves out of business every three years. What we do is profitable, but as we succeed, margins decline. What keeps us effective is that I can see things other people can't. I'm very intuitive."

Karen's intuition may sound a little inexact, but it is deeply informed. "I get my information from all kinds of random things. I listen a lot. I browse the *Wall Street Journal, Wired, Gourmet, InStyle,* and a bunch of food, trend, and economic newsletters. Also, I feel it's an incredible advantage being a female consumer. I shop. I cook. I'm a single mom. I'm an entrepreneur. And I'm damned curious about everything!" She doesn't have tunnel vision.

Lori Hallock's business may seem as far away from Frieda's as you can get, but Lori and Karen are trading off the same strength. Delaire Inc. started life as the supplier of telecommunication components.

"We found our little niche when the economy was just starting to take off, 1994. We were distributing electronic components, and one thing about the electronics business is its cycle. It has a supply and demand chain, and when new technology is coming out, there is a lot of pressure on the supply side. What happened was that some of the parts I had been buying and for which I had a large supply had an order lead time everywhere else of 52 weeks! So they became a hot commodity. Twenty-five-cent parts were selling for $8 or $9. But even at that price you couldn't get them."

Bear in mind that Lori Hallock is not an engineer or a technologist. She describes herself as a traditional housewife who goes home every night to cook dinner for her husband and look after the household.

"What happened was that I made some money buying and selling parts. Then I took a chance, and all the money I made as profit, I put into an order for parts I thought there would be a big demand for. It turned out I was right. We were able to turn my $10,000 into $250,000. So that's how I started my business!"

Lori showed me the mansions that dot New Jersey's shoreline, but she is proud of the fact that she and her husband have lived in the same modest house since they got married. What, she asks, are bigger houses except more rooms to clean? She has lived in this part of New Jersey—Bruce Springsteen territory—all her life. Asbury Park, Long Branch—about an hour from New York. Apart from her pristine BMW 740L, Lori bears no resemblance to the sharp-chinned CEOs that regularly grace the covers of *Fortune* and *Business Week*. She wears an overshirt, slacks, and maybe a little too much jewelry. She may not be smooth, but she is something far more important: She is intuitive.

You might say that Lori was just lucky (whatever that means) or has the heart of a trader (whatever that means), but her company kept beating the odds—not only when the telecommunications industry was booming but also when the New Jersey telecom giants around her started to topple.

"We were extremely successful during very good times. Then, during the telecom downturn, life got very difficult, so we expanded into some new products such as fiber-optic cable that is used to launch missiles off ships in the Iraq war. We started making subsystems for wireless communication just as wireless took off. We developed a line of fiber test boxes that is new technology. One of the reasons the product has been so big is that the cable market got into fiber, but the fiber was put there ten years ago. Now the cable companies want VOIP (Voice Over Internet Protocol) and all these things the lines weren't intended for.

"When the tech bust happened and huge companies were closing down, we had to get into other markets and try new paths, products, and technology. Where companies all around us were laying people off, we were retraining our people in military fiber."

What is so striking about Lori Hallock's Delaire, Carol Latham's Thermagon, Kimberly Bunting's Business Access, Doris Christopher's The Pampered Chef, Karen Caplan's Frieda's, and thousands of companies like them is that they are intuitive businesses run by women who have had the courage of their convictions. Often challenged and derided, they have nonetheless clung to their often unprovable insights. Their vision allowed them to see what market researchers hadn't even started to measure.

It is not just in what they produce that these companies are in tune with their times. Many are also farsighted in thinking about how they do their business. The Pampered Chef was able to grow so fast partly because its business model was predicated on there being a lot of women at home who wanted to get back into work but found traditional doors shut to them. Eager for financial independence, they found Doris Christopher's understated style of direct selling just what they wanted. As important to that company's success story as its products was its phenomenal success in recruiting kitchen consultants. Indeed, so successful were they that at one point Doris had to institute a recruiting freeze so that the company could catch up with its own growth. It is a rare company that has more suitable applicants banging on its door than it can process.

Paige Arnof-Fenn had a different vision when she set up Mavens & Moguls. She had enjoyed a successful career first on Wall Street, then running the Olympic Coin program, and then as a senior vice president of marketing at Coca-Cola. But she had had enough. She and her husband had been commuting for years and wanted to settle down together in the same town. She wanted more freedom, but she didn't want less stimulation. She found that many of her fellow senior marketers felt the same way. They had had tremendous success in corporate America but didn't want to live there anymore.

"So I had this idea. I thought: If I put all my best marketing colleagues together, we'd have an incredible powerhouse. But there's no way on earth that you'd ever get them all together under one roof, partly because some of them live east, some west, and some in between. Also, they don't want to work *for* anyone anymore. They know too much!" She laughs.

Mavens & Moguls isn't a typical marketing firm. It's a virtual firm. Companies who use their services get marketing teams with more experience and expertise than they would ever find in a single agency. Each team is assembled according to project needs rather than office politics or billable hours requirements. No one works *for* anyone; they all work for themselves and for the team.

"I just think this is the shape of things to come. Where you have very talented people with a lot of expertise, you also have people with a love of autonomy. Traditional corporations can't

hope to keep them on a leash. That's their problem and our opportunity. It has gone far better than I ever imagined. At first I
wondered if I was just kidding myself, pretending I had a job
when really I was just freelance. I wondered if I'd ever be able to
keep the pipeline full enough to keep everyone busy and engaged. In year two, we tripled our revenue, and the business was
growing steadily. In year three, we tripled again, and the concept
was scaling successfully. Then I started to panic. Could we maintain the quality and culture that we were known for if we tripled
again this year (year four)? It's a nice problem to have!"

Paige's instinct was right on two scores: She caught the mood
of her fellow marketers, and she also judged correctly that her
market was ready to try a business relationship that differed from
the conventional agency. In fact, her clients were desperate for it.

"Everyone's very polite, and no one likes to say this openly,
but there was a tremendous amount of cynicism about the agency
relationship. All that overhead! The glossy offices and expensive
addresses and the whole nine yards. And the sense that as a client
you were getting wound in tighter and tighter—not for your
own good but for the agency's good. It felt unbalanced and quite
manipulative. With Mavens & Moguls you get a lot of successful
people who are taking on work that they love. They could be
doing other things. They don't have tons of overhead to cover.
They just want to do great work. Technology makes it feasible,
of course, but the growing independence and freedom of talented
people makes it run."

What Paige is doing with a cadre of talented individuals,
Irene Cohen is doing on a massive scale across corporate America.

"What I saw happening was that companies were more and
more project driven. More and more money and people were
going into project work, but if the people were hired through

agencies, all the money went to the agencies. Where it was *not* going was into benefits, but it was the benefits that the bright, sharp people wanted. So here were all these bright, sharp people who were being paid on a project basis and getting no benefits because they were temps! It was criminal how much they were losing. Because the companies didn't want to make long-term commitments to them and wouldn't take them on full time, they were paying the agencies very well. They were spending a lot, but the money wasn't reaching the talent. It was a fundamental problem: The company wanted part-time commitment and paid too much to agencies while no one was looking after the people.

"I thought there had to be a way you could get benefits and work and not have to commit to one company and where the company doesn't have to worry so much or pay quite so much. So I said I could make that happen. What happened is that these people—lawyers, accountants, tech people—are all on our books as employees. We provide their benefits, and as their employer we send them out to companies where they work on projects. It doesn't cost the companies any more—they still have the freedom and flexibility they need—but the people also get the benefits they need.

"What's really great about this is that there's a huge pool of talented, experienced professionals who don't want to work a five-day week anymore or want to work nine months of the year. They still want to use their talent and stay in the game, and now they can do that without having to commit to a company forever. Most people who've worked for one company want to do something else, but they don't want to have to give up everything. Our model lets them have the best of both worlds."

Irene Cohen can see the employers' point of view: They need a flexible workforce and qualified people. They don't want to make lifetime commitments. She can see the employees' point of view: They want flexible work hours and secure benefits, but they don't want to make lifetime commitments, either. She has been able to empathize with both sides at a time when there is a crying need for both to be reconciled. If that weren't enough, she is catching a wave of disappointed retirees.

"The other part that is getting bigger is the retiree population. They realize that retirement isn't what it's cracked up to be. How many hours can you spend on the golf course? Where can you get the same satisfaction that work gave you?"

With clients like Merrill Lynch, Pitney Bowes, and Nortel, FlexCorp is growing by leaps and bounds. The first year they handled a payroll of $14 million. Last year it was $65 million. This year Irene thinks they may need to "cool it for a while."

"When you go into a corporation and ask how many contingency workers they have, they don't know because there are so many. Some come through agencies; others get paid by departments that have hired them on a freelance basis. It is a hidden workforce. But that all changes when they hire us and the managers begin to realize that this won't cost them a bundle of money and it will save everyone huge headaches. It is the shape of employment to come. It's here. It's amazing."

As Irene Cohen describes the logic of her business model, much of what she says seems obvious. The fact that this is the fifth company she has run says something about her ability to understand business, but when she first broached the idea for FlexCorp, she met nothing but rejection.

"The idea started a few years ago. I'd sold one business, but I didn't want to leave. So I asked if I could stay on to build this one, and they said I could. I got a back office and four people, and I built it in three years. They hated the idea. I wanted them to come in with me, but they wouldn't. They just didn't see it."

The empathy at which women excel is a double-edged sword. On the one hand, their instincts are frequently dismissed precisely because they are female. When did you last see intuition, empathy, or an understanding of zeitgeist in a business plan? These things are, as Baron-Cohen pointed out, "inexact" in a business world that clings to exactitude for comfort. Excellence in business is regularly equated with hardheaded logic and reason, with command-and-control rationality. Empathy and intuition fly in the face of the numbers-based, quasi-scientific model of business that dominates business schools and business journalism. The problem with having an understanding of zeitgeist is that everyone can't see what you can see. It works *because* it's ahead of its time, and often so far ahead that there's nothing you can point to to prove you are right. By the time you can, it's too late. Many of the female entrepreneurs I've met remind me of Cassandra, who was condemned to see the future but have no one believe her.

Recent research shows that this respect for instinct and empathy is a strikingly female characteristic. While men rely primarily on facts and logic when making decisions, women use *both* kinds of thinking. "Although women business owners are nearly evenly divided between left-brain (logical) and right-brain (intuitive) decision-making styles, they are significantly more likely than men owners to be right-brained decision makers (53% vs. 29%)" says the Center for Women's Business Research.[7] "The highest-ranked factor influencing women entrepreneurs when making business decisions is being sure they have all the relevant information and data available. Second in importance is whether or not the decision is consistent with a strong gut feeling." What this means is not that women are irrational—far from it—but that they combine rational thinking with instinctive thinking to make their choices. They use the full capacity of their brain to understand where they are and what to do. They do not expect only one form of thinking to be adequate.

The triumph for women is that when we have the courage of our convictions, we can be very successful. Our ringside seat at the business circus gives us a vantage point that others should envy. This is a more pertinent skill today than ever before. We operate in a business environment characterized by discontinuity, where the skills required to succeed are very different from those needed in an earlier, industrial age. In *A Whole New Mind,* Daniel H. Pink explores at length the kind of mind needed to succeed in this new business order. The qualities he elucidates are strangely familiar and feminine. Does that mean, asks Pink, that we all need to get in touch with the feminine side of our brains? Yes, he answers, it does. It doesn't mean rejecting the systematizing side of our brains; it doesn't mean rejecting discipline and focus. But it does mean that we need to start according these female strengths serious respect. They aren't soft. They're very difficult. Women have these skills in spades.[8] They drive our success. Attention must be paid.

Pink goes on to argue that what our age requires is what he calls "the androgynous mind." It combines discipline, focus, detachment, and systematic thinking with playfulness, empathy, and design. When I think of all the female entrepreneurs with whom I've spent time, I'm struck that most of them have emphasized how hard they've worked to develop their formal, rational skills. They take it for granted that they have the other stuff, the stuff that is so much harder to learn. They have androgynous minds by necessity.[9] A woman entrepreneur may not know that, and in my experience she is modest about it. But that's what she has.

Carol Latham was right about polymer semiconductors. Chances are there is a little bit of Carol inside your laptop today. She proved her colleagues wrong and reaped significant rewards for her conviction. But of course women who are in tune with the zeitgeist never stop seeing things, so she's interested in something new now.

"The thing that really interests me now is batteries. As we think about alternative fuels and energies, batteries are key. The whole problem with batteries is heat. How can you store all that energy without getting hot? What really burns me up is that we're giving all our battery technology to China—now, when it is the wave of the future! We have to do something about this, and I have some ideas."

3. Niche Is Nice
(and Margins Are Marvelous)

The American writer James Baldwin often talked about luck. When I produced a TV profile of his life, his frequent references to luck provoked my question: What do you consider to have been the bad luck in your life?

"To be born black, ugly, and homosexual" came the reply.

So what, I wondered, had been his good luck?

"To be born black, ugly, and homosexual."

Baldwin knew that what look like handicaps can turn out to be gifts. It is a lesson that women learn, too, which is just as well since the obstacles confronting women business owners are severe. Most banks won't take us seriously; venture capitalists scarcely know that we exist. Among institutional equity investments, women-owned businesses received only 9 percent of the deals and a scanty 2 percent of the dollars.[1] It isn't just in corporate America that women and the talents we represent are invisible.

We have little money and less confidence, and are less likely than men to believe we have the skills to run a business.[2] After years of operating in business environments we don't really fit into, it is scarcely surprising if we feel a little wary. The banks aren't welcoming us with open arms. The stories of women business owners almost never make it into the financial press, but there are plenty of people to remind us of the failure rate.

So where's the good luck? Lack of financial muscle, fear of failure, and lack of visible role models steer women away from the mass market and into niche markets. Which it turns out is exactly the place to be.

At a time when launching a mass market consumer product is estimated to require no less than $50 million, women are smart to stay away: The mainstream is a great place for new companies to be buried. These entrepreneurs are also smart because real growth is no longer found in mass markets. The last twenty years have seen the splintering of the market into thousands of niches to the point that many market analysts argue the mass market no longer meaningfully exists.

The rise of niche markets has been fueled by the rise in individualism, which pessimists call the demise of community. According to this social-economic trend, we do not seek to be part of the gang but to express ourselves as the unique individuals we are. We no longer want to wear clothes to fit in but to stand out. We don't want to be dressed head to toe in clothes from the Gap but instead to combine a Gap top with a Prada skirt and an ethnic bracelet—all underpinned with H&M underwear.[3] The same applies to men. The same applies to corporations whose servicing needs are every bit as specialized as the individual's need for self-expression.

Technology has fanned the flames. The conjunction of individualism (which makes us want something individual) with technology (which promises the power of mass customization) has resulted in unbelievably demanding customers. They argue, in essence, that since technology gives you the ability to provide perfect tailor-made goods and service, why shouldn't you? Such customers aren't satisfied with generic products, ill-informed staff, or casual service. In business terms, we now eschew the dark department store staffed by a few sleepy clerks who don't know the merchandise. We are more loyal and prepared to spend more in the boutique that remembers who we are and doesn't waste our time with wholly unsuitable suggestions.

The best way and the only way to serve such demanding customers successfully is through niche businesses that know their products and their customers with an unprecedented level of intimacy. If you can make the most of that intimacy, you can charge a lot more for your service.

Joni Walton's success owes everything to her niche. In 1989, she worked in customer service at Diagnostic Medical Instruments. Every day she fielded requests from clinics and medical technicians asking for medical supplies—not huge machines but all the accessories that made those machines effective. But DMI didn't sell those products. Joni hated disappointing customers every day—to the extent that finally she set up a unit that answered their needs. But when DMI was taken over by Burdick in 1993, they declared their intention of dissolving the business that Joni had created. That business is now the core of Danlee Medical Supplies, which sits in a quiet business park just outside Syracuse, New York.

What Joni did was find a niche, medical supplies, and then work hard to satisfy it. In doing so she uncovered all kinds of markets she hadn't known before, such as nurses, mental institutions, and veterinarians. But best of all she found that her product expertise was so outstanding, and her understanding of her customers so exceptional that her service could command a high margin. "Our customers are with us for a reason. We really know them and are very responsive to their needs. If there's anything they need that we don't have, we get it. And they pay for that. They're also very loyal, which allows us to build outstanding relationships with our vendors so that they give us good prices. When our competitors' margins typically run at 20 or 25 percent, we can get a gross margin of 42 percent or even higher." (Bear in mind that the average margin for Fortune 500 companies is 6 percent!)

Joni's company is so profitable that every six months she is asked if she will sell it. Its chief attraction is not its revenues but its profits. "I think profit is a lot more important than revenue. With profit you're making money. With revenues you're just making work."

Joni graduated high school but never went to college. She and her husband moved to Syracuse in search of greater opportunity. At the time all they owned was a black-and-white television and a lime green Chevy. She is cautious about her company's growth—you won't hear Master of the Universe business speak coming out of her mouth—but with healthy margins in a multi-million-dollar company, she can afford to be understated.

Rebecca Boenigk is another college dropout CEO who has discovered how powerful niches can be. Ostensibly, her Neutral Posture company is in the furniture business, but as the manufacturers of ergonomically designed chairs, they are in a particular subset of the furniture market. That can make it hard to know whom to sell to. "Sometimes," she concedes, "the corporate purchasing group may not be the best way in for us. They're not always that responsive. The most responsive pitch is the ergonomic one. It takes someone who knows ergonomics to understand the benefits of our chairs. We think of what we offer as a medical chair for those already injured or those who don't want to be injured. Repetitive stress injury is significant. Companies who've already experienced claims certainly see what we are offering."

To many a bank manager, that would sound so hopelessly specialized as to spell disaster, but not to Neutral Posture. With customers like UPS, Intel, and Lockheed Martin, the company has clearly proved the value of the niche it created. Its specialization is what accounts for the fact that while the furniture market as a whole has seen revenues drop by some 40 percent over the last three years, Neutral Posture has been able to keep their revenues steady. As the economy picks up, they are poised once more for substantial growth while the rest of the industry is repairing the damage from years of losses. "We think we survived because of ergonomics," says Rebecca. "We have a very good product, we are very lean, and we are very profitable."

Neutral Posture has been featured in the Inc. 500 list of America's fastest growing private businesses. So, too, has ISSI, the scientific engineering firm that Cecilia McCloy founded after she quit her job over dinner. "We've grown about 400 percent over the last three years, which is great and also really hard. We are actually trying to control our growth now because what happens to so many businesses is that they overextend themselves. And the kind of work we do is very tough; we have to be at the top of our game to do it well."

Cecilia talks lightly about work that includes some fairly mind-blowing projects. Her niche is doing engineering that requires significant degrees of innovation, creativity, and farsightedness. "We had a contract where our technical expertise was used at Stone Mountain in Georgia. There's a big confederate bas relief sculpture there. Because it is outdoors and carved into the mountain, it's been weathered for quite a while now. And they're starting to have a problem with the rock face. So the problem we face is: What do we need to do to save this for two hundred years? It's an interesting contract."

Part of ISSI's strength derives from the fact that there aren't many firms that can handle problems of this kind, and the problems aren't small. "We've been working on a high-level radioactive waste program in Nevada. It's cool because it means we have input into a climate model for the next ten thousand years. Nothing man-made can last that long, so we've been doing a lot of work around that. What happens if the water table goes up? Goes down? What are humans going to be like, and how do we tell them not to go there? These projects are important to the energy industry and to the world."

Cecilia's market is a classic niche market: It's narrow and very deep. This means she can develop towering expertise in it. She knows the kinds of customers she's talking to; she knows the kinds of employees she needs to recruit. One of the very hardest parts of running any business is getting a tight enough definition for it that everyone knows where to focus. Inside and out, it is important for everyone to know what you do and what you don't do. That is the power that niches can deliver.

"Sure it is a niche," says Pat Loret de Mola about her business, "but what a niche! The market as a whole is worth $2 trillion. That's more than equities and bonds *combined*!"

Pat's company, Trade Settlement Inc., builds and runs back-office software for settling all the details involved in syndicated bank loans. Imagine the gruesome tedium of closing on your house loan. Now imagine thousands of those daily—loans spread across multiple banks. Then imagine a technology platform that automates the process. That's what Pat's company does. It is parked temporarily in contract offices near New York's Ninth

Avenue. It doesn't look like Wall Street or feel like Wall Street, but Wall Street is where its impact is being felt.

No one does what Pat's company does because it is complex, hard, and because the syndicated loan market (where Pat has spent most of her career) is like the rest of banking: dependent on trust that takes a long time to nurture. Banks like Citigroup and Bank of America can't entrust this kind of work to just anyone, and they've learned to be wary of Internet start-ups that claim to understand their business.

One of the many smart things that Pat did when she started the business was that she didn't rush out and hire a posse of software engineers. She didn't have the money, and she also didn't know anything about technology. This might have seemed like bad luck, but it wasn't. "I knew my limitations. I had no idea about technology. I had no time to hire a technology team because I was so worried that Reuters would beat me to the market with a competitive product. And I had no money, either. So I outsourced to a Canadian group at a time when the exchange rate was very attractive." Not surprisingly, Pat spends a lot of her time on planes and in meetings. She wants to know and understand everyone involved in the decision to work with her product, to ensure that it ends up making all of them look like stars. It may be high-tech, but it is also highly personal.

In not hiring developers, Pat kept it very clear in her own mind and in everyone else's that she was not building a technology company but a financial services company. The people she hired have financial services backgrounds. Her customers are all financial services companies. Her niche market definition has spared Pat the siren call of so many technology companies: With the potential to do anything, they end up with no definition or focus at all. Hundreds of tech start-ups have died that way as they lurched from the consumer market to the corporate market and back again. Pat's niche has kept her focused so that everyone knows what Trade Settlement does.

At $2 trillion, Pat was chasing a rich market that knew her well. Her involvement in a tightly defined industry gave her a high profile. That means she has a seat at the table where the decisions that drive her industry are made. "I'm very involved with the industry association, which means that I can help them understand some of the technology issues. It's easy for them to say, 'Let's make this standard effective from tomorrow,' because they don't really have a sense of what's involved in implementing that standard. So instead you teach them by introducing a comments period and training them not to mandate standards without that process. That way I can prevent conversations that would otherwise be catastrophic to my business."

When she started, there was nothing that promised Pat success. She had to learn to do without all the nice perks of working for big Wall Street firms: no Town Cars, no Four Seasons, no assistants. Today she sits in a rented conference room, glancing occasionally at her BlackBerry, still every inch a banker but a different kind of banker. One that has created value and not just transferred it. One that has discovered new territory and claimed it—not for her firm but for herself and her employees.

It is a model that Diana Pohly knows well. She was an early pioneer in custom publishing. The Pohly Company publishes magazines for airlines, trade associations, real estate developers, car manufacturers, and any business that wants to build customer loyalty through sophisticated, targeted content produced in a manner consistent with the corporate brand. She took over the company in 1996. "Custom publishing wasn't really an arrow in the quiver of marketing professionals when we started. Marketers would think of TV, radio, packaging, and print, but not custom publishing. Then, in 1997, the Custom Publishing Council was formed. Getting involved right out of the gate was crucial because it was so important to define custom publishing in our terms—as a marketing tool and not as an arm of publishing. Because I have been instrumental in defining the whole category in my terms, I'm seen as a leading company. We've developed a high profile within the industry and have a lot of big-brand, high-value clients. We are now perceived as one of the top five. Because it was a new category, there was a real chance to dominate it."

Get in early. Define the niche to your advantage. Dominate the niche. That is what Diana Pohly, Pat Loret de Mola, and other canny niche marketers have figured out. Owning a category isn't about size; it's about influence. It's a lot easier to have influence, even when you're young and small, when the category itself is well defined.

When you combine niche positioning with an understanding of zeitgeist, you have a pretty staggering mix. Nadine Lange's Open Scan took an ugly niche—exception mail—at a time when the electronic processing of payments was in its infancy. As electronic bill payment grew, so, too, did all the mistakes and irregularities in bill payment. When there were only a few exceptions, fixing them manually wasn't a big deal, but once you get thousands or hundreds of thousands of them and fixing each one costs up to $6 apiece, automating the solution becomes an urgent priority. Generalists just didn't understand the problems well enough to be effective, but Nadine did.

"I freak myself out at times thinking I started something so new. What I find even more amazing is that no one else is doing it. That amazes me the most. Why not? They think it is easy.

They get into it, and it isn't easy. But every year we get smarter about it. Dirty mail.

"We were up at five this morning visiting a mailroom. I took the whole team there to watch. These poor guys in the mailroom were dealing with 200,000 to 400,000 items a day, and all the data entry was being done by hand! I wanted the team to see every inch of the nitty-gritty. That's how we understand it better and better. It is our only focus.

"It is great that we focus on something so defined. The problem we solve doesn't get bigger, but the market does! That's the beauty of niche markets. Others are just starting to get into it, but they don't know what they're doing. And we've been working with this stuff and with our customers for years now."

John Franco is Open Scan's brilliant chief technologist. He has been digging into this very unsexy problem for years with an appetite that's unabated. "I stay close to tech support and testing, so I hear every complaint about the software and everything we've done well. I get a lot of ideas from that. Every customer we work with, I find a way to improve something. As the technologies that we use get better, the whole system gets better."

It is a beautiful model. Every time Nadine or John listens to a customer, they find ways to improve their product, which then benefits every customer. There is probably no one in the world who understands the problem and how to solve it better than Nadine and her team. To date their biggest customers have been state agencies processing child support payments, but they're also talking about handling retirement funds, mutual funds, and even church donations. "It's incredible," admits Nadine. "These huge churches. The ministries collect a million dollars a day in fifteen *thousand* payments, and they haven't automated it yet!"

That women home in on niche markets is often seen as a sign

of weakness. Why, I'm often asked, aren't women more ambitious? The question itself is a giveaway; it implies that ambition has to be about size, not depth; quantity, not quality. And of course the question reflects a misreading of the value and opportunity that niche markets provide. No, they don't lend themselves to the grandiose promises of the kind so beloved by investors. And, no, you won't hear from any of these CEOs the kind of chest-thumping braggadocio that characterized many a failed software start-up which, wanting to do everything, ended up doing nothing very well.

The good news and the bad news about niche markets is that they offer precious little space to hide. They also offer the one ingredient absolutely essential to an entrepreneur's success and more important even than funding: focus. When you know what you're doing and what you're not doing, and when every single person in the company knows that, nobody wastes time or resources on work that isn't mission-critical. When you know your customers as well as you know yourself, they come to depend on you and become your greatest evangelists. With great products, service, and customers who love you, you can build repeat business, marvelous margins, and a reputation for excellence.

I don't call that unambitious.

Part 2

It Ain't What We Do, It's the Way That We Do It

4. The Value of Values

Forty years ago Thomas Watson Jr. wrote, "The basic philosophy of an organization has far more to do with its achievements than do technological or economic resources, organizational structure, innovation, or timing." Philosophy matters more than technology or money? Values count for more than innovation? More than market timing? How could the son of IBM's founder think such a thing?

Well, maybe he listened to his mother, because one striking characteristic of women's businesses is how central values are to everything they do. Sure, women can talk big growth numbers and revenue projections, but it's never the start or heart of their conversation. When a woman talks about her company, she is far more likely to talk about its philosophy, about the purpose underlying her business, which turns out to be intimately connected to values. Values matter in business because they drive the brand, reinforce the market position, and show managers how to make coherent decisions and trade-offs. When they help companies hire more assuredly and treat a workforce with consistent respect, they save money by reducing staff turnover. Those are the instrumental, operational assets that having values confers on a company.

One way to discern a person's values is to watch the decisions made under pressure. The same is true for businesses. The last five years have given us a spectacularly good opportunity to see what company values surface in a crisis because every business has its 9/11 story. We all have memories of what we did that day. But what business leaders did on the day itself didn't speak the loudest. It was what they did in the months afterward, against the backdrop of economic gloom and despondency, that revealed their values more starkly.

Brenda Rivers's Andavo Travel was particularly badly hit. At the time, Andavo was a $100 million travel company that served corporate travel clients. After 9/11, everyone stopped traveling.

"Well of course 9/11 was a crisis. It was the end of the world. We were refunding more money than we were taking in. How long can you keep doing that? A good entrepreneur is good in a crisis, and this was a crisis, but there was no one to reach out to because everyone else was in a crisis, too!"

Brenda, an elegant woman whose southern belle style belies a sharp brain, is a lawyer by training. She founded Andavo with her own money and enjoyed its exponential growth, but all she'd ever known were good times. This, she thought, should stand her in good stead. She had a line of credit with the bank that she'd never had to use. It was up for renewal in October.

"I needed it now for payroll. I knew we had a big new client coming in January, so the question really was: How to stay alive until then? I went to the bank to renew this line of credit that I'd never drawn on—and they turned me down! The bank told me, 'We don't think you'll survive,' and they turned me down."

Being in a service business, Andavo didn't have physical assets; all it had was staff. Like most CEOs, Brenda had always said that her employees were her most precious asset. She talked easily about how she valued them and how they lay at the heart of her motivation in growing her business. But now those values were put to the test. How far was she prepared to go to protect her people?

"I had only one choice. I had to go into my personal funds, all the money I'd saved. And I cashed in my retirement. It was a huge risk, but I knew in my heart I was doing the right thing. I couldn't stomach the idea of going in and telling my staff to go home. I had a lot of single parents working for me. It was all about the employees. I wasn't worrying about whether I was going to lose everything. If I'd done that, I'd have been immobile. It was all about the employees, and there was just no way I was going to lay them off."

That year, 2001, was the first year Andavo had ever lost money. The following year they broke even, and they've been profitable ever since. Their revenues now are higher than before 9/11.

"It's really funny," Brenda said with a laugh, "because I found out recently that the employees' perception of me through all this was that I had everything under control! But I was freaked out! Inside, I was scared to death."

Brenda may have been scared to death, but she wasn't scared out of her core values.

"For me, running a business has always been about making a difference to my employees. The people who work here *know* that they're valued, and I love it. I have people who left Amex and other top companies (where they were making a lot more money) just to come here. But they love working with me. Last year we gave 10 percent of our profits to different charities. Ten percent! Every year I tell my employees to take a day's paid leave and go help someone. *I get to do that!* So, yes, 9/11 was horrible, but 9/11 didn't change my core values. It strengthened them. It brought me closer to my employees.

"What comes back to me over and over again are what it takes to be an entrepreneur, the basic values. And these are: One, you can't be afraid of risk. That's smart, calculated risk. I jump in. I do my homework. I don't lose sleep. And two: You have to have faith in your employees."

Most of Brenda's major competitors in the travel industry had huge layoffs. Others cut back on health insurance. In the U.S. economy as a whole, over a million workers lost their jobs in the three months following 9/11. And many companies—including the world's biggest company, Wal-Mart—cut back on employee health care benefits. These companies may have said that people were their most precious asset, but they didn't mean it. Their actions revealed their values.

Values come in and out of fashion. In the 1930s, the CEO of New Jersey Bell, Chester Barnard, maintained that it was the leader's job to shape and guide the values of the organization. He described good managers as *value shapers* and contrasted them with the mechanical manipulators of reward systems and short-term efficiency.[1] In the 1960s, at IBM, Thomas Watson Jr. argued that the biggest difference between success and failure could be attributed to how faithfully it adhered to a sound set of beliefs. In the 1980s, Tom Peters and Robert Waterman, in their landmark book *In Search of Excellence,* argued that the one truth they derived from their study of business excellence was this: "Figure out your value system. Decide what your company *stands for."* What is so interesting is that each time one of these business thinkers argues the primacy of values, it sounds like a cry in the wilderness. And, of course, at the turn of the millennium, companies such as Enron, Global Crossing, Adelphia, and Tyco showed what happens in companies that have no values at all.

Values are the beliefs that guide decisions. They are what people work *for,* the thing beyond cash remuneration that gives their work meaning and purpose. In a business world characterized by discontinuity, it is values that provide continuity. They prevent decisions from being and feeling random. They provide meaning and coherence to employees, customers, and stakeholders. They build a narrative that makes sense.

Authenticity, which has become a buzzword, is not itself a value. A CEO who is authentic may make greedy, corrupt, incoherent decisions if that is the kind of person he or she authentically is. Believing, as Brenda Rivers did, that your employees are the most important part of your business is a value. It determined her post-9/11 decisions, which is why she felt she didn't have any choices to make. It means that Andavo stands for something. And the company's employees and customers believe Brenda because her actions have been consistent with her values.

This doesn't mean the company is static. Since 9/11, much has changed at Andavo. "Change is how we work," says Brenda. "I love change. We just keep looking for ways to improve things. A client you've had for twelve years can't be treated the same way for twelve years, or you'll lose him." Thomas Watson argued that you can and must be prepared to change anything *except* your values, and that is what Brenda has done—and she has done it because she doesn't know any other way to work. It wasn't a deliberate decision; instead, I think 9/11 revealed to her just how deep her values went. Deeper than perhaps even she had imagined.

What strikes me about so many of the women business owners I've met is that they put values at the center of their businesses, not because they've read somewhere that it's a good thing to do but because it never occurred to them to do otherwise. They approach their companies in the same way that female executives approach their careers. They seek work lives and home lives that are integrated, not separated. They are eager to fulfill different roles but not to compartmentalize their lives, separating work values from home values. They want to organize a myriad of activities around consistent principles, ideals, and philosophy. Values for women are not an afterthought tacked on to the business once it is successful. What the company will stand for is sometimes in place before the entrepreneur knows what the company will produce.

In upstate New York, near the Canadian border, there is a sleepy little town called Lyons Falls. You probably haven't heard of it unless you love hiking, in which case you might have passed through it on your way to the Adirondacks. In the summer it is hot and wet and smells of pine trees. Last year the area had the heaviest snowfall on the East Coast. There's a closed-down paper mill, a sub shop, a hardware store, a bar and diner, and a gas station. There's nowhere to go for dinner, and if you have money, there's not much to spend it on.

But Lyons Falls is the headquarters of a very remarkable company started by Doreen Marks when she was sixteen years old. Out hunting with her father one day, she slipped in the mud. Her gun got clogged up, and she had to go home to clean it. Her day's hunting with her dad was ruined. But Doreen was and is a pragmatic person. Why, she wondered, did she have to lose a day's hunting? Why couldn't she clean her gun there and then, and resume hunting?

So Doreen sat down and invented her first gun-cleaning kit. She made it so that it would fit into a shoe polish tin. She tested it in the field and kept refining it. At sixteen she was too young to be admitted to gun shows, so she put on high heels and lip-stick, and her dad sneaked her in to look around. That's how Otis Technology was born. It now manufactures and sells "the world's finest gun care systems" to the U.S. military and to the world. The proud holder of over thirty patents, Otis sets the standard for cleaning guns. What Otis stands for, and what Doreen has always stood for, is quality.

"This company is twenty years old, and I've been running it for more than half my life," recalled Doreen. "When I was grow-ing up, I wouldn't buy something just to buy it. I'd save to buy the best. So when the idea evolved, I wanted to make the highest quality because the regular stuff that was available was so poor. You get what you pay for. We aren't cheap gun-cleaning kits. We are the Rolex and Mercedes of gun cleaning. I didn't want this to be a company that made cheap stuff that broke. Some merchants wanted that, but I said no. They just wanted planned obsolescence. I don't buy into that philosophy."

What Doreen does buy into is the philosophy that says you do *everything* to the highest possible standard. "We don't have dissatisfied customers. We give a lifetime warranty. The standard strength for cleaning rods is 50 pounds, and 150 pounds breaking strength. We manufacture to a breaking strength of 700 pounds. We've had one returned in twenty years, and that was because it was dropped in a fire. We have a product that is so good and so reliable that we are never afraid to answer the phone."

"The kit fits into the back of the gun. It's very compact and can be stored and carried to places where lives depend on it. It has a lot of safety features. We've designed it so you can't clean a loaded gun. We send free parts if they break. Everybody in the factory and in customer service knows that if they can't satisfy the customer, the call comes to my office.

"Because of our philosophy about quality, we were accepted internationally before we were accepted in the United States. Europeans see guns as a legacy, something you look after and inherit, so quality is very important to them. They just see our brass fittings, and they know."

It is the company's obsession with quality that drives it to innovate. In fact, the rate of innovation at the company is so fast that they now bring in an intellectual property lawyer twice a year to audit their new products and file new patents; otherwise, they might forget. "The M4 has a collapsible stock, so the old cleaning solution doesn't work. Nick invented a kit that goes in the hand grip. It's the smallest cleaning kit in the world. It also holds a battery for night vision, and we're working on adding GPS so you can find missing soldiers and weapons."

Now in her mid-thirties, Doreen is a single mother of two teenage girls. With waist-long dark hair and sporting shorts, she looks more like an intern than the CEO. For all her casual dress, she is perfectly groomed with an impeccable manicure and a spotless leather handbag that wasn't bought in Lyons Falls. But quality isn't just Doreen's passion, it's everyone's. Anyone in the company can stop manufacturing at any point if he or she sees something faulty. And everyone thinks about how to improve the products and the processes. Her brother Nick now designs both the products and many of the machines that manufacture the products.

"To be a government supplier you have to be able to warrant that your supply chain won't be interrupted. That means you can't rely on parts that are made in or shipped from countries that are politically sensitive. Of course, that's a really hard thing to do. Nick now designs a lot of our machinery so we can make most things ourselves. And even when we've bought machines from other companies and other countries, he's designed machines to make any spare parts we might need. We can guarantee that we'll never have to interrupt production."

Having this level of innovation inside the business guarantees the quality of both the product and the service, and it also helps cash flow.

"Being self-sufficient in manufacturing makes the cash flow a lot better. Before, we'd have to order components ahead of time, and they'd take our orders only if they were in huge numbers. Then we'd have lots of cash tied up in inventory. Now we have just-in-time manufacturing, and we don't have to babysit a lot of suppliers. That has turned out to be critical for us because with the war we've had a huge increase in orders, and we couldn't wait and depend on others. The government can't buy this from China." Otis has won awards for its products and also for its on-time delivery record.

Otis Technology began in Doreen's parents' kitchen. She continued to refine her product while she went to college, and afterward she alternated waitressing with making gun-cleaning kits. As the company grew, Doreen did every single job in the business. There is no aspect of its operation that she doesn't know and hasn't done. Eventually, the business outgrew the kitchen and moved to a horse barn. It outgrew the barn and moved into an old lumber yard. It doesn't look like the headquarters of a world-beating company, but it is.

In July 2005, everyone was getting ready to move into a brand-new, purpose-built facility that is a cathedral to manufacturing. Biometric entry devices keep it secure, and underfloor heating keeps it warm. Heated sidewalks ensure that employees won't slip during the long, harsh winters, and heated drains ensure that they won't freeze. The factory has a mile of compressed air lines, and air in the facility is exchanged every two minutes. Doreen spent $40,000 painting the ceiling white, not because she had to but because having a white ceiling makes it a more cheerful place to work. Low-energy lights turn themselves off when there is no movement. The copper pipes in the boiler room have been polished and shellacked; they are machinery, too, so they've been treated with love and respect. Even the janitor's closet has been designed with care, and Doreen went in one weekend to try out the janitor's cart, cleaning doors. In the kitchen there is room for massage chairs, and the cupboards await customized doors that are being made by the Mennonites. The driveway was moved an extra two acres in order to distance it from the outdoor picnic area.

All the machines have names, and Doreen knows what every one of them cost and what it does. Some were made by Nick when he was in high school. Now that he has his robotics degree, he'd like to redesign one of them, but it still works fine, trimming seventeen metal cleaning brushes a minute. Otis is using robotics more and more, not to reduce the workforce but to eliminate dirty, dangerous jobs. The brush-trimming used to be done by hand, "but the women who did that job ended up with so much metal embedded in their hands, they couldn't get through metal detectors! Now we do it with robotics. The brushes are pretty much like mascara brushes except that the fibers are metal. The machine even kicks out faulty brushes. We don't want to decrease jobs; we just want to use people better. That is what robotics is about."

Nick has retrofitted a machine designed for trimming fiber-optic cable to cut their cleaning cables. That has eliminated a big source of carpal tunnel syndrome. And all manufacturing waste is recycled. "We want the land our families live on to stay clean," said Doreen. Crossing the parking lot, she picked up a candy wrapper. She wasn't exaggerating when she said that you could eat your lunch off the factory floor.

Every machine, every design is a value statement, and so are Doreen's decisions. "Kmart wanted us to do a lower quality product in plastic. We wouldn't do it. It just isn't what we are about. We are always striving to do better. I don't think we've been completely successful yet; there's so much further to go."

Doreen brings the same commitment to people that she brings to her products and manufacturing processes. "We offer Fortune 500–style benefits. If you've worked for us for a year, we pay 100 percent of your health care coverage. We offer a 401(k) and flex time. When parents have award ceremonies at their kids' schools, of course they can go to those. You work here for your family so families have to come first. I'd really like to open a child care facility. We have sixty employees here with thirty-five kids who need looking after, and we'll be hiring more."

Otis has never had a layoff. Many of the employees do four to five different jobs. No one knows anything about the business when they start, but they learn fast. "We have a lot of diamonds in the rough here, lots of people who will come up to management level in years to come."

Doreen's values deliver clear business benefits. The commitment to quality positions her definitively in the marketplace. All 165 products are built to exact specifications, and every customer knows what to expect. Quality is the brand, and quality is the company's unique selling point. Moreover, the Otis values save money. The company has very little staff turnover, and recruitment isn't a challenge. The employees are proud to work for Otis and wear the Otis polo shirt by choice.

When I asked Doreen how she saw the next twenty years,

she didn't spout growth rates or revenue numbers. She talked again about her values. "I want to make sure that we keep the philosophy going and that we all grow personally. I want to make sure the foundation is firm for the future. I want to keep to the dream."

Some two hundred miles south of Otis Technology is a better-known company that you'd expect to be very different. Eileen Fisher doesn't hunt, and the clothes she makes are not designed for the rugged outdoors. Eileen and Doreen are very different people in almost every respect but one: They both believe in the primacy of values.

"Probably more than anything else," said Eileen, "I believe in telling the truth and keeping it simple. They're spirit principles, the things that keep your spirit alight."

As in most businesses, there is a connection between the values of the founder and the values of the business. Eileen Fisher first started designing clothes out of a passion for simplicity, because she found the experience of shopping overwhelming.

"I found clothes so confusing. I loved clothes, but I hated to shop. I would go into stores and feel sick, overwhelmed by choices. Trying things on just made me confused. I wanted it all to be simpler, easy, and comfortable. I wanted to feel good, be myself, and not have to fuss."

Twenty years later the company's purpose is a crisp reflection of that early vision: "To inspire simplicity, creativity, and delight through connection and great design." Of course there is a very tight fit between the values, the brand, and the products. The clothes are simple, rarely patterned, and very easy to take care of. They are creative and connected because they're designed as a system; they work together in a myriad of combinations. Buyers say they're popular because those combinations can be as personal, as conventional, or as idiosyncratic as the individuals who wear them. And they're very kind clothes, respecting the many shapes that women come in.

Eileen believes in simplicity with a real passion. She lives in a big house outside New York City that, for all its size, is very plain, in quiet shades without a single picture on the wall. It isn't ascetic; the living room window that frames a stunning view of the Hudson is drama enough for one room. But the overall atmosphere is one of simplicity, exactly the opposite of the chaos of color and design that sickened her when she went shopping. The insistence on simplicity goes far beyond style. Talking to Eileen Fisher and seeing the way she moves and thinks, you begin to see that keeping it simple is the way she makes sense of her world and of her business.

These core values have enormous repercussions for the company that Eileen Fisher has built. The belief in simplicity leads to a belief that there shouldn't be a conflict between work and home life, either in the clothes (which should be able to transition seamlessly from one venue to another) or in the workplace. Creativity and delight aren't just about cool clothes; they're about making the clothes in fabrics that are physically comfortable, using means that are ethically comfortable. The company is one of only three in the United States to comply with the workplace standards administered by Social Accountability 8000, the standard-bearer in their industry.

"We got very involved in SA8000, which has standards that cover health and safety, wages, and working ages, and working hours at factories around the globe. We pay attention to the environment. We are willing to invest more in that area. Our employees tell us they recognize the importance of this."

The fashion business isn't famous for its commitment to values. In some circles, fashion is considered the polar opposite of values. But Eileen Fisher is a contrarian. Fashion experts claim there are only two markets: high end, very expensive designer clothes, or low end, cheap and temporary clothes. But Eileen Fisher makes elegant garments that are neither cheap nor expensive. They suit both young and old. They are appropriate for work and in the evening. The passion for simplicity lies at the heart of this, but so does one other commitment: "to produce only what we love."

Eileen would be the first person to tell you that holding these values and finding ways to implement them in a fast-growth business is difficult. There have been times when she felt there was a lack of alignment between the values that the company espoused and the day-to-day experience of working there. But Eileen never let herself off the hook; she never shrugged and accepted that that was the price she had to pay for growth. She kept looking for ways and people that would help her comb the values all the way through the organization. She believes in simplicity, but she knows that achieving simplicity can be very complicated.

"I remember speaking at Pace University about the company values, and someone asked, 'How do you make sure that the values are happening? You have hundreds of employees. How do you know it is happening the way that you want?' I was honestly stunned by the question because I knew I needed to do more than just put the ideas out there. I knew the company wasn't really organized; it was patchy. I asked myself: How do you work holistically at this instead of just patching up the problem?

"When the company was little, it was fluid and it worked. When it got big, it became mired in lots of contradictory structures, and no one knew what it meant anymore. We were being wishy-washy and didn't make decisions the right way. We were going away from ourselves. I knew I had to find some people who could help me think about how to make the company work."

Eileen's values hadn't changed, but the business had grown so fast that their presence within the company was erratic. New employees, importing different values, had unwittingly created a hybrid mess, the opposite of the simplicity she craved. Over the years Eileen has worked hard to reorganize both the company and her leadership team, to keep it simple and synchronized even as it grows bigger and richer. She has hired new people for new positions, such as Susan Schor, who is chief culture officer, and Amy Hall, who is director of social consciousness. She has also developed a clear statement of the company's purpose. To make sure it isn't bland propaganda that no one pays attention to, the purpose is broken down into practice guidelines that are employed as the basis for all annual reviews. All these developments testify to how seriously Eileen Fisher takes the challenge of working the values holistically through what is now a very big company indeed.

She herself remains engaged in ensuring that both the product and the way it is produced continue to articulate core values. "The essence of the product," she said, "is the essence of the practice. The product has to make explicit what has been implicit in the business."

Diana Pohly has spent her life in client service companies. The Pohly Company is the first one she has owned. She has thought long and hard about what it stands for, not least because some of her past experiences have shown her the dangers of a values vacuum. She bought the company in 1999 when the owners decided they wanted to get out of the custom publishing business. She inherited a team and a culture riddled with distrust.

"It was a real have-and-have-not company. You had eight

people in these massively gorgeous offices with huge windows, and everyone else was stuck in cubicles like rat mazes. It bred resentments, and there was no team spirit. The prior president had imposed no requirements, no goals, no business plans. Everyone loved him because they didn't have to do anything! When I came in and told people what they had to do, they hated it. They weren't used to it! There was a lot of gossip and sniping—a very distrustful environment. It was just not my management philosophy."

This was the first time Diana had ever run her own business. She took out a large loan from the parent company. She needed clients. She needed money. But what she needed first was to put her management philosophy into action. She might be under pressure, but values came first.

"I'm a very honest person—probably more so than is good for me sometimes—and when I took over this company and told people what was going to happen, I was amazed when no one believed me. They didn't believe me because they weren't used to being told the truth. It didn't matter what I said; the old company culture meant there were people who didn't believe it and would go out of their way to tell people what I really meant. But, of course, what I really meant was exactly what I'd said!" She laughed.

The Pohly Company values emphasize honesty, trust, hard work, and excellence. Diana said these are inseparable, but trust is most important. Teamwork, which is how everything in her business is done, cannot function if team members aren't honest. They won't trust one another if they aren't all being honest and working equally hard. If they don't share a commitment to excellence, they won't trust one another. It is a tall order, but as anyone who has worked in a dysfunctional team knows, it is grounded in a deep understanding of how collaboration does or doesn't happen.

Many of the client service businesses that I've observed have run aground because everyone involved in a project had competing goals. The art director wanted to win awards. The account director wanted to run up billable hours. The account manager wanted to be recruited into the client's marketing department. The copywriter wanted a higher word count. Interests weren't just misaligned, they were at odds with one another. In those conditions, trust is a pipe dream. It is a scenario that Kevin Miller, Pohly's chief creative officer, knows well from his time in a leading New York agency.

"You'd have done better working in a gravel pit! You always got silos. It was all political. There was no sense that what you did mattered to anyone or that anyone would tell you the truth about anything. But this place—well, this place has always felt honest. What you see is what you get. No one is goofing off. It's not about jockeying for position, it's about improving your skills and building the business. So we have standards by which we measure everything, from design to edit to how a meeting went. Diana put process into the company, so it was clear who was accountable. No hiding. No finger pointing. Because if you can't be trusted to be accountable, you're not here."

"Core values here include a real commitment to team, which means people have to trust one another. That means open and honest communication. We think about values here all the time, in everything we do, and I've spent a lot of time thinking about how to make them real," said Diana. "After all, everyone can *say* them. I hate posters of mission statements, so I kept asking myself: How do we use our values and inculcate them into our everyday operations?"

As her business grew and thrived, Diana came to see that it is very hard to impose values on those who have none and probably impossible to change the values of people who don't share yours. And until you translate values into processes, they don't mean a thing. That is what changed the hiring process at The Pohly Company. Yes, the company hires for skills—you can't hire designers for a communications business who don't know Photoshop—but those who are hired must also share the company's core beliefs.

"It really bothered me that we were interviewing for tasks, but nothing in our interviewing determined how people related to our values. Now we have ten value statements, and when we interview candidates, we evaluate them against those statements. If they don't score high, they aren't going to fit in. The work we do is so team oriented that if people don't share the same values, they simply won't work well as a team."

If you don't subscribe to the company's values, you don't get in. And if your behavior doesn't articulate those values, you can't stay. At The Pohly Company, annual reviews are conducted by five peers. The message is loud and clear: What matters is not just what you achieve but how you achieve it—that is, whether your work puts Pohly values into action. It is a tough process and a long one, and it is at odds with the routine assessments many companies pass off as annual reviews. Pohly evaluations are demanding not only for the employee being evaluated but also for their peers who have to think long and hard about how they collaborate.

This may sound rather grim, but the company isn't. After all, another core Pohly value is a sense of fun. Diana herself is a very relaxed, jolly woman. She is serious but not solemn. People look forward to the company's "Friday at 4" meeting, not just for the wine and beer but for the easy accolades and thanks that colleagues pass along to one another. Diana teases the editorial director about a headline. Everybody cheers when one magazine made $90,000 over its goal, and everybody groans through the customary requests that the kitchen be kept cleaner. New business is celebrated, but so, too, is the announcement by Mark, the new employee, that he has finally learned how to transfer a phone call. Martin concludes the meeting by teasing Liz and Karen about wearing the same color and by revealing that today, Arbor Day, was first made a federal holiday by that little-known environmentalist Richard Nixon.

Articulating and enacting values inside the company is an achievement, but what happens when those values are tested outside the company? After all, The Pohly Company depends on clients for its revenue. What happens if the client doesn't share the same Pohly values? How do these values and that sense of shared purpose stand up against a toxic client? Diana maintains that, inside or outside the business, the core issue is always trust.

"Where things can be mismatched the most," said Diana, "is where there isn't the level of trust that we need to make the relationship work. The client has to trust that we have the expertise they don't have. If the client can't trust that, it just doesn't work. In fact," she went on, "I was about to resign a client just the other day, but the person didn't trust us to do better work than she could do herself. She was a control freak. Fortunately, her boss already saw this and saw that the relationship was heading in the wrong direction. He therefore made the decision to remove her and keep us."

Would Diana really walk away from a major piece of business just because the client valued control over trust? It is a question anyone running a service business must face: What matters more, client dollars or company values? The decisions a business leader makes in situations such as this say more than any mission statement ever can.

"The creative and account teams have to trust that I will choose the people who work here over a client and the money. In the past I have resigned clients because of their lack of trust, where the net result was a master-servant relationship. It is lip service if I don't stand up and say: This is a clash, we have to get rid of it. If I believe that we work with each other on trust and we work with clients on trust, then I have to stick to that. Otherwise, our whole system falls apart. I can either resign the client or lose my talent."

Values have made Diana Pohly's company stronger, more talented, and more productive. The company is held in high esteem by its clients and competitors. Some of Diana's employees when talking about her were literally lost for words as they tried to articulate how different their work was from anything they'd known before. The company values make it easier for everyone to know what to do, how to prioritize, and how to collaborate. But values can't protect any company from the outside world.

Kevin Miller recalled that "9/11 was awful for everyone. But for us it was unbelievable. Our biggest clients were Continental Airlines and American Business Travel Association (ABTA). Everyone was looking at their budgets and thinking: Do we really need a magazine? And staff here flipped out because everything stopped for a couple of months. You stop making the money you were making, and you have no idea what is going to happen next."

What happened was that Diana suggested to her senior management team that they make 10 percent paycuts across the board, with an additional 5 percent cut from their own pay. In these circumstances, teamwork had to mean shared pain. It also meant shared learning. She sent staff on negotiation courses, to teach them how to strike better deals with vendors. She provided the entire staff with details of the company finances and she asked them all to help restore it to profitability. She refused to make any layoffs. For her, the key challenge was to stay in business any way she could, while not losing the trust of her employees. Each of these goals was tough; together, they were formidable.

But Pohly core values did more than remain intact. The commitment to hard work, honesty, and teamwork were more relevant now than ever. At a time when everyone was frightened and confused, those values never wavered but, instead, showed everyone how to get through the crisis. By the end of 2002, the company had eked out a tiny profit. The following year, at a company offsite, Diana handed out hundred dollar bills to everyone, to thank them for all their hard work. It seemed a small reward for a grim year—but then she also announced that she was rescinding the pay cuts and awarding merit raises. The Pohly Company has not looked back since. In 2005, they announced an expansion plan to take them into media sales, market research, and design communications.

Values inform brands, reinforce market positioning, simplify complex decisions, and clarify client relationships. When values are used to identify appropriate employees and eliminate the inappropriate, they help companies hire more effectively and reduce costly turnovers. These are real, instrumental, operational advantages. It is easier and more efficient to work in or work for or work with a company that knows what it stands for. Values reduce friction.

I think the value of values goes further still. Values give people a sense of purpose, a sense that they are contributing to something bigger than themselves. Psychologists and philosophers distinguish between hedonic happiness, which is the pleasure derived from food, drink, and things, and eudaimonic happiness, "which is not derived from bodily pleasure, nor is it a state that can be chemically induced or attained by any shortcuts. It can only be had by *activity* consonant *with noble purpose* (my italics).[2] Companies that are based on values create the conditions in which that activity consonant with noble purpose can occur. Such businesses can make people happy and productive. Sociologists chronicle the decline of community and the loneliness of individualism.[3] But a company that stands for something can provide that sense of belonging to something bigger than oneself. Does this replace community? Not entirely, but it does position a company as a forceful contributor to individual and social good. Few people in the world may have heard of Lyons Falls, but the town would be a lesser place without Otis, and its employees know that they make an impact in the world through their world-class products.

It strikes me that the women I spoke to didn't discuss their companies or the way they work as if they were discussing machines. This isn't their mental model. They talked about their companies as living organisms and sometimes as though they were talking about a child. This was not because they regard employees as children—they absolutely do not. Each woman looks upon her company as a living creature challenged to survive within a dynamic, demanding environment. That organism needs to develop the right way. It could go wrong if not constantly corrected. It benefits from good relationships and can be corrupted by bad ones. These women are determined that their companies will grow to be healthy, responsible beings whose contributions to the world will be positive. And each of these women thinks her job is to teach, nurture, inculcate, and support the values that make this feasible.

Eileen Fisher discovered the hard way that articulating and believing in values isn't enough, especially as the company grows. The values must be constantly reexamined and incorporated in every relationship, every product, and every interaction the company undertakes. Diana Pohly discovered that those values must hold up against external values and against catastrophic events. Doreen Marks knows that values are what keep the company growing.

In all the years I have spent running companies and talking to my fellow female entrepreneurs, I've been struck that every one of us talks not so much about the business we are in but about the kind of business we have or want to have. Many women I know didn't start with a product idea or a service concept. They started with a philosophy, and that philosophy has guided them to their market. Men may dismiss this as soft or sentimental, but I don't think it is anything of the kind. I think that most women start with values and that this turns out to be exactly the right place to begin to build value.

5. The Power of People

Values inspire people with a sense of purpose and a sense of belonging. Such inspiration is not negligible. Gains of 30 to 40 percent are evident when managers are able to inspire high employee commitment. On a broad scale, the correlation between *Fortune* magazine's list of the Most Admired Companies (for investment purposes) and their list of the 100 Best Companies to Work For suggests that happy, motivated employees make for better long-term investments. Analysis of financial results from publicly traded companies suggests a 20 percent premium for those businesses with high employee moral. On a more granular level, enthusiastic workers have been shown to increase the quality of their work by huge percentages—up to a 75 percent reduction in defect rates.[1]

Investment firms are starting to see how much this matters. At Calvert Investments, Barbara Krumsiek makes quality of life, sustainability, and diversity part of the criteria for any business that her funds invest in. She says it is simple: If you want to put your money in the best companies, you have to find the businesses where the best people are treated with fairness and dignity. To that end, the company incorporates social analysis into its investment process, actively encouraging companies to adopt the best practices and investing in disadvantaged communities. Believing that people count, they put their money where their mouth is. Recently, they issued "The Calvert Women's Principles," a global code of conduct for corporations. Barbara believes in these principles, but she also believes that her funds won't be competitive if they don't push companies to develop productive, equitable cultures. With more than $10 billion under management and years of top Barron's rankings, Barbara Krumsiek is under a lot of pressure to keep proving what she believes to be true.

Cultures matter because they can either inspire more commitment or less. And they have to be managed conscientiously; they don't just evolve. (As Peter Drucker once remarked, "The only things that evolve by themselves in any organization are disorder, friction, and malperformance.") A company's culture can be positive (inspiring high orders of enthusiasm), neutral (tolerating indifference), or negative (sanctioning malevolence), but every company has a culture, whether it means to or not. What is striking about female entrepreneurs is how seriously they consider culture. For them, building a healthy culture and a happy workforce is not a human resources task, and it isn't an optional extra.

In 2005, three consultants who had spent a lifetime studying organizational effectiveness came together to pool all the information they'd gathered from millions of employees over the years.[2] They found that the challenge for companies did not come from malevolent employees—there are actually very few of these—but from indifferent employees, of which there are many more. How, they asked, could companies turn indifferent employees into enthusiastic ones? First, they argued, "we must understand what workers want. Then we must give it to them." What did they want? Fairness, the opportunity to achieve, and a sense of community. I didn't find a female business owner who had read this study, but any one of them might have written it.

FAIRNESS: EVERYBODY IS SOMEBODY

"A few days ago, one of our drivers, Lon, fell off a ladder. It turned out he broke his legs and was also bleeding from his nose and ears. That didn't sound good to me. He has a daughter, and I knew she had been only fifteen when she found her mother dead in bed of heart disease that no one knew about—and that was two years ago. So there she was, only seventeen and all by herself looking after her dad. We found some free tickets to fly her two older sisters out so they could be at the hospital with Lon and be there to help his younger daughter look after him."

Maureen Beal isn't a social worker, and she isn't the head of human resources. She is the chief executive of one of the largest van lines in the United States, and she was talking about one of her drivers. Maureen is a tiny woman, under five feet tall, with sleek salt-and-pepper hair and immaculate grooming. I can't remember when I last saw so much power concentrated in such a tiny space.

Maureen Beal has experienced double-digit growth every year since she took charge. But what jumps out at you the minute you walk through the door is her intense concern for individuals. Her workforce may be widely dispersed, but Maureen believes that makes it even more imperative to make people feel they count. Wherever they are based, the company still cares about each of them.

National Van Lines was started by Maureen's father. She worked for the company as a switchboard operator—"Remember when they had those switchboards with the wires you plugged in?"—and later as a bookkeeper.

"I grew up with these people. Some of the drivers I knew as a little girl—when I was twelve—are still here. They were my friends. They knew me by my nickname, Sissy, and I still know all the drivers by name. If they're in Chicago, they come by and say hi."

Maureen moved to California for a while in the 1970s. For the first time she wasn't working for her father's company, and she learned a lot.

"When I worked in manufacturing," she recalled, "I learned what it was like to be an employee. You'd go to the canteen, and everyone would be sitting around saying, "If only the management would listen to us." I learned that you have to share information with the employees so they don't start to imagine things and wonder what's going on."

Maureen listens to people, and she remembers them. She remembered not just Lon but his daughter and his late wife and his other two daughters. Remembering her employees in such detail makes it very clear that at National Van Lines everyone counts. But if it were just Maureen who listened, that wouldn't be the culture of the company. Her listening habit has become part of the company's culture because Maureen has created disciplined ways of institutionalizing it throughout the company. She has taken something personal and turned it into processes. For example, National provides training for their drivers—not only when they join the company but for as long as they're there. Some of the training is mandatory, but a lot of it isn't. The training goes way beyond what's necessary; it becomes an important way for the company to reach out to the drivers who are spread across the country. It is so highly regarded that it has become a powerful lure for drivers to leave other van lines to go to National.

"The first thing we have to do is convince them that they'll benefit from the training—not the van line, but them personally—because if they're taking time off the road, that's revenue to them," explained Jorja Coulter, who runs the training sessions. "We show that it makes their lives easier, reduces claims, and speeds up payment. We teach them effective crew-leading. One year we focused on wrapping and building tiers effectively. This season we focused on safety. It's all the same: communicate, communicate, communicate.

"It's training, but it's not one-way training. It helps them, and it helps us. Drivers come more than once. We publish the schedule, and drivers can pop in if they are in the area. They come back because they learn from other drivers. They love the camaraderie. Some like to be the center of attention, and this gives them a forum. They bring problems and want me to help solve them. They know they can get things fixed based on what they tell us. I've had drivers from other companies say, "Wow, I didn't think you could teach me anything, but I didn't know this."

The company trains and listens to the drivers at the same time. Jorja may be a vice president and a driver may be a driver, but they listen to each other with equal attentiveness. "In other companies," said Jorja, who has worked for some of those other companies, "drivers can talk only to dispatchers. They can't make suggestions. No matter what they say, they feel they don't have a voice. But here they have a driver council and can talk to individual VPs. They have a personal connection to the organization." And it isn't just lip service. Issues brought to the council have changed the way National conducts its business.

"It sounds hokey," conceded Maureen, "but we treat the drivers like people. They don't want to be treated like just another driver ticket on the board. For example, at one driver council it turned out that they hated making deliveries to downtown Chicago because it was such a tight squeeze and so congested. So we bought a straight truck for downtown deliveries. They can come here, unload into the straight truck, and go into town. They love it!

"Other companies don't listen. One of our competitors doesn't even have a parking lot at the head office for trucks, so the guys can't go in and talk. Here, they come in, they talk to the people in operations, and they see me.

Communicating with drivers takes special effort because they are so widely dispersed. But National pays just as much attention to its office workers.

"Leroy worked for us for twenty-five years, then he retired. Six months later he wrote asking if he could come back part-time, and he did. Sometimes he'd fall asleep while he was writing. We all worried that one day he'd hurt himself falling out of his chair. The safety director warned me about it. I replied, "Okay, let's buy him a chair with arms so he can't fall out." Finally, when he was eighty-four, he re-retired. That's just one example of how we stand behind our people.

"The employees know we won't throw them out. Like Dottie. She's had chemo, but she's on full salary. Some days she comes in, and some days she doesn't. But the last thing you want to worry about when you're going through that is your paycheck! I know I tend to mother them, but I don't think that's all bad. They have to feel that the head of the company has empathy. I've learned to be comfortable with my own style. When you have great employees who stand behind you because you've stood behind them—that's a great feeling."

Maureen may mother them, but nurturing individuals is how she nurtures the business as a whole. Thinking of it as a living organism, she devotes time and attention to the well-being and development of that organism; she is tireless in looking after those who contribute to its growth. Her attention is egalitarian, but it isn't unconditional. She will protect those who strengthen the business, but she'll expel those who don't. Even her own brother.

"I had two older brothers, and when I was growing up, if one of them needed some milk, my mother would ask me to get it for them. She'd say to me, 'Sis, can you get Frank his milk, please?' And he'd be sitting right there! And Frank let me!"

All three children worked for the company. Six months before he died, Maureen's father told her he was leaving the company to her. The younger brother, Ron, was fine with this; he loved computers, and as long as he had a meaty IT project, he was happy. But Frank wasn't happy.

"He liked the *idea* of being president, but he didn't want to do the work, so he undermined me. It was terrible. He had to leave. It's a terrible thing to fire your own brother. It was not nice. But I was fair."

It cost Maureen a lot to get rid of her brother—a lot of money, a lot of time, and a lot of pain. It sent an essential message about the company that deeply informed its culture. Maureen's kindness isn't soft; it is part of a contract. She helps you; you help the company. Reciprocity is fundamental. We stand behind you if you stand behind us. Everybody matters, but that also means that there are no favorites.

Maureen is scrupulous about people, about money, and about quality of service. The company's expansion has allowed her to consolidate the culture in its processes and also in its physical presence. Like many of her fellow women business owners, Maureen has placed great store by articulating the company's respect for its workforce in bricks and mortar.

"This building used to be in a late 1960s time warp," she said with a laugh as she showed me around. "I wanted the employees to come into the building and be proud of it. And I wanted it to look to the agents as though we were a prosperous company—not extravagant but doing well. And being a typical woman—you know, you buy the dress and then you need the shoes and the handbag—once we did part of the building, we then had to do the floors and the walls and the sewers and, well, everything. Now we are redoing the kitchen and the lunch room, and installing all new windows. It's important for people to have a nice place to work."

It is easier to articulate such egalitarian principles when times are good, and they've been very good since Maureen took over; over 20 percent growth every year for five consecutive years. That kind of growth is a challenge, but the bigger challenge to a culture is market change, especially the kind of change that the Eliassen Group faced in 2000 when the Internet sector, on which so much of their growth had been based, went bust. Unlike many of the other companies in this book, Eliassen couldn't avoid lay-offs, but Mona Eliassen realized that, at such a moment, culture was more important than ever.

"Your company's culture gives you a framework in which to work—a set of rules, a way of doing things, a behavior. I learned the hard way that, at times like that, you have to stick to those rules more than ever. The first layoff, I was as sick as a dog, so I left it to the HR people. They said: Do it fast. I let them, but I thought it was brutal. I don't care what they say—it's a horrendous way to treat people. The employees were just blindsided.

"March 2001 was the second layoff and the last one. This time we did things differently. We had monthly staff meetings, and I told people to be prepared. I did not want them to be blindsided again. I shared all the numbers with them so they knew where we stood, and I said that if we didn't hit those numbers, we would have to do layoffs. People thanked us! We could give severance; we could give people time to find other jobs. I think it's just horrendous when one day people are sitting there working for you, and the next day they've disappeared."

It was a far cry from software companies like PeopleSoft, which delivered layoff notices by voice mail. What Mona realized was that, bad as it was, how you conduct a layoff conveys a powerful message.

"We called it Back to Basics—back to working hard, having fun, but keeping the culture in place," recalled Mike McBrierty. "We didn't change any of the core values. What we cut were some of the higher-level positions that we didn't necessarily need. And we didn't cut the compensation for any of the employees. In the leadership team, compensation is based on hitting numbers, so in good times we do better than the industry, and in down times we take a hit. But we didn't impact the staffers who run the business.

"When we were going through the layoffs and thinking of all the things to cut, Mona was really forceful about not cutting things that would impact the culture. She knew that even though we had to make layoffs, we also had to preserve the company and its culture. We still had fresh fruit in the kitchen every week. A dry-cleaning company came in, and a massage person brought her table in. We had visiting nurses come and give flu shots. Cutting these things wouldn't have saved jobs, but keeping them kept us together. Mona is pretty sensitive to issues of other people in the workplace. She is empathetic to what other people go through."

Every person I met at the Eliassen Group talked about the massage table and about how retaining it kept their spirits up. Small and apparently trivial details like this contain a potent message. When, in 2004 (not even in a recession and while sitting on a mountain of cash), Microsoft stopped supplying fresh towels in their locker rooms, it sent a message.[3] When, at the worst moment of their history, Eliassen hung on to its masseuse, it sent another. Everybody counts. The company still cares.

"I remember at Wang when they had problems, they took away the tissues in the bathroom! Something you kinda need. It was ridiculous," said Mona. "For me, culture is not the only thing. But the more I run a business, besides having a market to sell to, I think it is the most important thing."

Eliassen does fresh fruit and massage. Otis Technology does cookouts and exercise rooms. At Neutral Posture, Rebecca Boenigk provides school supplies for employees' children at the beginning of the school year. These apparently small gestures, available to everyone regardless of rank or seniority, convey powerful messages about equality and fairness.

Equally important, if not more so, is the provision of benefits to employees. At a time when most companies have been cutting back on these—Wal-Mart reduced its health care coverage to employees, and IBM reduced the number of dependents covered by its health insurance—women's businesses have been loath to follow their example.[4] In fact, you are more likely to be offered a choice of insurers and pension plans if you work for a woman. What this says about the company is that it is serious when it talks about valuing its people.

Perhaps the greatest test of all of whether a culture is fair or not can be shown in its hiring. Men's companies hire predominantly men. Women's businesses hire men and women equally.[5] The same applies to their boards of directors: Women appoint men and women equally, while men favor *themselves* at a rate of three to one.[6] This may be because, having been on the receiving end of discriminatory hiring, women are determined not to repeat the mistake. But all the women I've talked to hire diversely not because of any ideological grudge but because they genuinely value and enjoy a diverse workforce.

"We cater to a market that's men and women," said Diana Pohly. "We live in a world that's men and women. So of course we want men and women here. It is more creative. It is more fun. It makes us smarter."

STRETCH: PEOPLE, LIKE COMPANIES, LOVE GROWING

Mistelina Quinones was one of Carol Latham's recruits in the early days of Thermagon. Her husband knew Carol's son Jim and heard of the company that way. Ten years later, she sits as a supervisor, in front of a poster that celebrates Loyalty. It is clear that Carol is immensely proud of her—beaming would not be too glowing a term—and it's equally clear that Mistelina is very proud of what she has accomplished.

"Before I came here, I was just a housewife with three kids, and I needed the money. I dropped out of school in eleventh grade, but they trained me. The atmosphere was great, very friendly and very quiet. You could say anything. It was almost like a family."

So happy was she at the company that she recruited other family members; at one point seven members of Mistelina's family worked for Thermagon. The company gave them opportunities they had never found anywhere else—chances not just to work but to learn, study, and grow.

"Working here has improved my life," said Mistelina proudly. "It has given us the chance to prove ourselves."

At Carol Latham's Thermagon there is still a classroom inside the company offices. It dates from those early days when, unable to afford the time or the expense of finding experienced employees, she hired inexperienced Hispanics and Latinos and trained them for the new careers.

"The Cleveland school system provided us with teachers, and we taught them English, math, and computer skills on company time. It has been a pretty neat thing. Then they'd recommend someone else, and you knew there was no way they'd recommend a person if they didn't think it was someone they could be proud of."

Carol changed lives. Mistelina didn't just recruit members of her family; she stayed, studied, and advanced through the organization. Today she runs the forming department where Thermagon's materials are shaped. She still loves getting her hands into the thermally conductive putty, which is a bit like bright purple cookie dough, but now she manages a crew of eight people with quiet authority. Not one of them, she said, has ever given her trouble. Mistelina isn't the sort of person that most CEOs would have spotted as management material. She herself said there was nothing in her background that indicated she could do this. But Thermagon's need and Carol's support showed her how much she was capable of.

"I love working here. I would never have gotten the same opportunities anywhere else. When I came here, I really wanted to better myself, and I have. And now that the kids have grown up, Mom can do her own thing." It speaks volumes when an employee describes doing her job as "doing her own thing."

Thermagon is housed in an old brick building that used to be a label factory. It is decorated with original works of art and a Noguchi table; the reception area overflows with awards. One senses from Carol that the impact the company has had on peoples' lives means as much to her as all her industry and technology accolades put together.

"I call it the icing on the cake. I wish I could say I had the foresight, but I didn't. It just happened. We promoted lots of people into positions of responsibility. We have a lot of women, a lot of minorities and blacks, and to have that chance to improve people's quality of life and to make their lives better is rewarding. I recognized what a great chance I had. It wasn't a great vision—but I suddenly saw the opportunity.

"For several years running, Thermagon got onto these lists of companies doing good in the inner cities—one run by *Inc.* magazine and another by Michael Porter and Harvard. It was great to be in there—I got to meet Magic Johnson!—but when I looked at some of the companies, I realized they were doing good but weren't doing all that well. Whereas we were doing the inner-city thing *and* we were making money!"

Carol, and many women business leaders like her, does more than take an interest in her employees and treat them fairly. She doesn't accept that a company needs to choose between altruism and growth. She doesn't look upon people as a net cost. She creates the opportunities that allow her employees to grow, and that makes the business grow. She presents them with assignments that are a stretch. She has confidence in them and provides the support they need to succeed. She understands that people work for a lot more than just money; growth goes both ways.

"I learned a lot from BP about what not to do. A word of encouragement can go so far. The people who have come here have really proved themselves. We helped them, but they did it. We rarely lose people. We take pride in treating people as human beings, not as human resources. The real reward for them is being able to grow as the company grows.

"I think the fact that I was a homemaker for eighteen years taught me a lot. You learn nurturing and multitasking. Also, during the time I was at home, I did a lot of volunteer work where you learn how to get people to do something for no reward. I don't regret those eighteen years at all."

"I like it better when it is harder. It is more gratifying when you succeed," acknowledged Mona Eliassen, and one suspects Carol Latham would agree with her. Fundamental to the culture of both companies is the recognition that business growth and personal growth are inseparable.

"It's an amazing place," said Eliassen's Peggy Murphy. "I'm enormously proud to be a part of it. When I was in sales, I wanted to be a bigger part of it and to understand how to run a business and help it grow. That has allowed me to grow a tremendous amount in handling people, both clients and the folks who work with me here. We are big into asking people three questions: What should I *stop* doing? What should I *start* doing? What should I *keep* doing? When I ask those questions and then listen to the answers, I sure do learn a lot.

"I've had three kids since I started working here, and Mona has been incredible to me about my schedule. I used to do four days a week, now I've come back full-time. But the point is that it was never forced. They said they trusted me to do a good job. It was stressful, but I didn't have the added pressure of their disapproval. They appreciated my schedule when I had to leave to pick up kids. They could have added to the pressure, but they never did. They helped me be successful."

And Eliassen is fastidious about recognizing success.

"We have the Pinnacle group: they all have their own goals for the year and if they hit their goals, they can go on a trip with their family, usually to the Caribbean. This year it's Jamaica. I wore a Rastafarian hat at the company meeting to remind them all about Jamaica—and everyone's on target so far!"

As she recounted this, Mona gave the impression that she was as eager as any of her employees to win the Jamaica trip. And months later she was proud to announce that they all did hit their goal, so everyone got to go.[7] But big annual rewards are not the only way that excellence is recognized.

"A few things I've done have been good. I ask people to send appreciation e-mails to people they appreciate. I do that every so often. In January I asked everyone to do it. Some came to me, and I read them; some went to whole teams. This one guy wrote this unbelievably eloquent e-mail about his team and what their strengths were. I'm big into the appreciation stuff."

"We reward people," said Dave McKeen. "At our monthly company meetings we hand out the Masterpiece award to non-sales and recruiting staff who've gone beyond the call of duty. Each month the winner gets $500. We have a parking space for the award winner right next to the door. We talk about the reason that someone was nominated, and everyone gets to vote. All the winners are entered into a drawing to win a week's trip to wherever they want to go. It's all about recognizing people for their achievement.

"Recognition is very important, especially for back-office people. In the past there were some tough relationships between back-office and sales people. Now we have a common goal. There is no good cop/bad cop stuff here. This is very different from what I've seen elsewhere, and I love it."

There's a big emphasis on growth in these companies, an implicit recognition that personal growth and company growth are inextricably linked. At Otis Technology, Doreen Marks insists that all her employees have to get a degree in something they're interested in. She helps them do it and welcomes them back when they're done. She wants to stretch people, and she wants to reward them, too.

"We've had people here for fifteen years," she told me. "When you've been here fifteen years, you get a trip around the world. We also do a lot of cross-training because it keeps people interested if they're always learning."

For the staff at Otis, personal development is closely linked to product development. Doreen is clear that she won't outsource production to low-wage overseas companies (and she would jeopardize her military contracts if she did). She competes, she said, through technology—by using or inventing the best technology she can find and deploying it creatively. What that means for everyone in the company is that they are constantly retraining and learning new skills.

"I learn every day," said Doreen's brother Nick. "You take the best part of everything you see and figure out how it can go together. We never stand still."

CAMARADERIE: EVERYONE BELONGS TO SOMETHING BIGGER

Every woman-owned business I've ever studied or visited has sooner or later been described to me as a family. The analogy is always used as a compliment. It covers a multitude of qualities reflecting the fairness, pride, and pleasure in achievements that these cultures articulate. (It may also show a certain amount of gender stereotyping in which every female founder is inevitably seen as the mother of the company.) Women's businesses, centered on values, create a strong sense of mission. Working for them feels like being part of a larger community that has a sense of common purpose uniting a highly diverse range of personalities and skills.

What is so striking about these companies, however, is that their employees, while clearly feeling nurtured, also feel stretched and challenged by goals that are much more defined and catalytic than in any family I've ever known. There aren't that many families that pore over cash flow as obsessively as National Van Line's Maureen Beal or that agonize over the best use of technology as passionately as Otis Technology. And I hope there aren't too many families that are as driven and goal-oriented as the Eliassen Group.

But what is important about the familial aspect of these cultures is that they do not polarize work life and home life. Just as Carol Latham doesn't think you have to choose between looking after the business or looking after the people, these women business owners do not believe you have to choose between having a career and having a family. Most of them have done both, and they recognize that their employees—women *and* men—want the same.

"It's important to me that we have a warm, inviting culture

here. When you walk in, you're offered a cup of coffee before you can get your coat off," said Doreen Marks about Otis. "We have lots of flextime. We're trying to provide child care. We want people here to think that this is part of their lives, not something that takes them away from the things they care about."

"We want people here to think that this is part of their lives" is a profound statement, one that is hard to hear—and even harder to see enacted—in most of the boardrooms of America. These women say it and mean it because, at least in part, they would feel uncomfortable taking for themselves something they weren't providing to their workforce.

At Eileen Fisher Inc., the integration of work life and home life lies at the heart of the brand, so it's not surprising to find that it lies at the heart of the culture. Each employee receives a $1,000 personal education benefit and a $1,000 wellness benefit. Yoga classes are held onsite to simplify the lives of those who would otherwise find it hard to squeeze Yoga into their day. Eileen believes that for her employees to be creative and productive, they need to be healthy, and she wants the company to help. But perhaps the most important way that home life and work life are integrated at Eileen Fisher is the least tangible: The company doesn't clock-watch. It doesn't measure creativity, productivity, or commitment by hours.

"I love this world, but I didn't come from this world," says Heather McGinley who has worked for Eileen since 1997. "Before I came here, I worked in the garment industry in places where you have to stay until ten o'clock at night—not for the work but for the sake of it because someone once said that's how you show you're serious. But the thing is, when you know you aren't getting out until ten, you kind of drag the whole day. Now no one here blinks when I walk out at five to pick up my kids.

"There's trust here and freedom for us to know how to get the work done. We can ask questions. Is this meaningful work, or is it work for the sake of it? Eileen is the first person to ask that. She's constantly questioning that. She wants us to maintain balance of life and work because that's how you stay creative."

Companies like Eileen Fisher are serious about growth, profitability, and sustainability. They believe that these are best achieved by breaking down barriers between work life and home life, by creating cultures that are flexible and strong enough to sustain both. Nurtured at work, employees have the energy left to nurture their own families—who in turn give them the energy and creativity they need to work well at work. Families reinforcing families.

Companies are communities, but Mona Eliassen's concept of community extends well beyond her immediate business. She runs a philanthropy committee that raises funds for any number of medical and social charities: American Diabetes Association, American Heart Association, Dana Farber Cancer Institute, Environmental League of Massachusetts, and Young Entrepreneurs Alliance, to name a few. And at Christmas the company sends care packages to American troops on active duty.

Faced with such a widely dispersed workforce makes creating a sense of community all the more important and all the more challenging to National Van Lines, so every two years they hold a convention in Chicago. All the drivers, agents, and employees of the company gather for three days of discussion and celebration. On Wednesday there is an opening party, on Thursday a conference about the business and where it's going, followed by another party at the Shedd Aquarium. On Friday night there's another party at headquarters, and Saturday night is awards night.

"It's a major event," said Jorja Coulter, who organizes the

whole thing. "It's a huge undertaking and sometimes, frankly, a little daunting, but it's a great way to bring everyone together and to show them what a huge contribution they've made to the business. Maureen gets to meet everyone, and they get to meet her. When you have people spread all over the country, it's really important to bring them all together."

A central feature of the convention always involves the marine artist Wyland, with whom National has collaborated since 2000. As he travels the country conducting coastal cleanups, his transportation and logistics are taken care of by the van line—whose trucks are covered in one of the artist's murals. Together, the company and the artist are working hard to find ways to teach children and adults to respect the oceans.

"I just love the work we do with Wyland," said Maureen. "I presented the awards for the Wyland Foundation, and I think it's a big deal for our company. They're very proud to be part of it, to know that they're contributing to something really great."

National Van Lines isn't just trying to save the oceans. Different teams in the company host breakfasts—at $5 a head—to raise money for the American Cancer Society. (So far, the chocolate, raspberry, and macadamia brownies seem to be the big hit.) They hold raffles and garage sales in their parking lot and have raised $20,000 from their one hundred employees. Maureen personally chairs ASPIRE, an organization that works with the mentally handicapped. As the mother of a handicapped daughter, she knows what such families face. What is important about all this activity is that it deeply informs the company's culture. It provides a level of employee engagement that goes far beyond putting in hours.

At Neutral Posture, Rebecca Boenigk finds that her ability to give back is a big motivator for both her and her employees. And she has learned not to keep that pleasure to herself.

"We're involved with many charities, but it used to be that it was just my mom and I who decided where the money went. Now the employees decide where the money goes. There's a charity committee, and every quarter they invite three charities to come and make a presentation to the whole workforce. Then the employees vote. The bottom one gets $1,000, the next one gets $2,500, and the top one gets $5,000. All the money comes out of company funds."

Although women's businesses are still smaller, on average they give as much to charity as other businesses, which means that they are giving a higher proportion.[8] Community is important to women, and they show it in the ways they spend their time and the ways they spend their money.

What strikes me about the cultures in all the women-owned businesses I've studied is that they provide all those things that academic studies say are essential if you want enthusiastic, committed employees: equity (fair treatment and interest in individuals), achievement (being given the tools and recognition for achieving stretch goals), and camaraderie (teamwork and a sense of community). But they provide these lavishly, applying a very broad interpretation of their employees' needs and going beyond expectation in fulfilling them. Maureen Beal's emphasis on listening and her ability to remember in minute detail each and every driver go far beyond anything a management manual would dare to instruct. The education that Carol Latham provided her inner-city employees was a success that even she didn't appreciate until later. And the sense of community that these companies have developed extends far beyond the employees, their families, and the immediate geography.

Much of this starts with the founder, but it's important that it doesn't end there. If it does, the leaders might have personal values, but their companies won't have cultures. What each of the women here has managed to do is extend her core beliefs about fairness, growth, and community into all of the company's processes so that they touch each employee all the time. When the beliefs extend into every corner of a business, regardless of the CEO's personal intervention, then you have a culture that breeds enthusiasm and commitment.

These company founders lavish time, attention, and money on their people because they know it matters. When they say that people are their most precious asset, it may be because in most instances people are their only assets. Lacking investment of any kind and shunned by banks and venture capitalists, the women leaders have to nurture their people. The business depends on it. It may be bad luck that the companies have so few hard assets, but it is clearly very good luck that they have more than compensatory talents in their leadership.

That these cultures feel so natural and unforced explains why founders and employees alike refer to them as families. It is also why, when women create these kinds of environment, their leadership is often described as mothering. The implication is that this somehow comes to women naturally, that it is a biological, not an intellectual, imperative. I'm not at all convinced that that is true; for one thing, there is far too much discipline in the way these women work, communicate, and scrutinize to suggest that they're just following some biological urge. I suspect that the analogy is used to undervalue the immense power of women's talent. If it is natural, then it doesn't take any skill, does it? Of course it does. It takes skill, energy, effort, conscious discipline, and relentless vigilance.

Nevertheless, there is a good cultural fit between what society expects of women—to be caring, communicative, encouraging, and fair—and the kinds of cultures that they build. When I first met Maureen Beal and was struck by the sense of power she exudes, I wondered where that came from. Now I think it comes from the perfect fit between who she is—a woman, a mother, a highly driven, super-smart executive—and the role she inhabits. There is quite simply nothing holding Maureen back. She isn't trying to please or placate anyone. She doesn't have to disguise or mitigate her femininity, nor does she want to soften her determination. She is wholly herself in each moment at least in part because she has discovered, through her company, that who and what she is works wonders.

Some twenty-five years ago Tom Peters, trying to define business excellence, wrote, "In the last analysis, it's really about culture. Now culture is the 'softest' stuff around. Who trusts its leading analysts—anthropologist and sociologists—after all? Businessmen surely don't."

Business*women* surely do believe in culture. They do a lot more than believe in it; they act on it. They put time, attention, and money into developing sustainable cultures that enhance the lives of their employees and their communities. Thinking of their companies as living organisms, they pay attention to making those organisms thrive. They know that a healthy, supportive culture makes communication easier, reduces turnover, inspires loyalty, and enhances teamwork, which is the source of their creativity. They know a strong culture gets them through traumatic events with goodwill and work ethic intact.

And they know they're very good at it.

6. Leadership as Orchestration

To reach the Eliassen Group, you first drive past dilapidated New England clapboard houses and then by the new generic office blocks. It is the eclectic architectural mess that is Route 128, the spine of Boston's high-tech industry. Companies along 128 come and go with alarming speed and regularity. One year, Global Crossing took over a plate glass monolith; the next year, its logo was replaced by the space available sign. It is a brutal ecology, as unforgiving and volatile as the Boston climate. One of my own companies faced onto 128, and nothing of the road's legendary luster could protect our inadequate software from the demands of an industry that wanted start-up innovation coupled with old-world stability. In a state that values history and heritage, almost nothing on 128 stays the same or lasts for very long.

This is just one of the reasons that the Eliassen Group is so remarkable. It is a software consulting and staffing company, which means it provides engineers and project managers to companies that are building new technologies. It has been in business for sixteen years, which on 128 is practically forever. It isn't run by a macho kid who loves fast cars and private planes. It is run by a mother of two with chronic fatigue syndrome.

"The disease is really a double-edged sword," said Mona Eliassen. "There were times when I slept twelve, fourteen hours a day. There was a time when I couldn't read for six months. But the good part of this is that it has helped me focus, and it has made me delegate. The beauty of that is it made the company worth more."

Mona is a slim woman who at first seems unremarkable. As you watch her, you gradually realize she is very beautiful. There is nothing in the way she presents herself that makes her stand out; her beauty just gradually reveals itself. Her brain functions pretty much the same way. Jargon-free and utterly unpretentious, it takes a while to realize how smart Mona Eliassen is, how intricately she connects ideas. Perhaps it shouldn't be surprising that her leadership style is similarly oblique.

"We have a very strong leadership team here. There are all different kinds of people with different strengths. I've worked on that. I've used everything I could find—every book, every seminar—to work on them. And now my leadership team will talk about *anything!*

"I was a great learner at school, and I try to apply that at work. I love to learn new things and how to make things bigger. I've always had a drive for excellence, and I knew I had to have a great team. I'm not threatened by their excellence; I like it!"

Mona is constantly finding books for the team to read, such as *The Five Dysfunctions of a Team* and *Good to Great*.[1] She knows that she needs a strong team because she can't be in the office all the time. This has clearly influenced her idea of power and how she uses it. It isn't physically possible for her to be a command-and-control leader, overseeing the troops and telling them what to do. But neither, one feels, is this how she would want to lead even if she could.

"The team is much smarter together than I could ever be alone. They have very different personalities. My VP of recruiting is a rock. He's never going to be a change agent, but he's going to keep steady when we're changing. My CIO takes a long time to make decisions; I'm much faster. But he slows me down, and I speed him up. I like different people; I like to learn from them."

Mona's leadership consists of her COO, three sales directors, the CFO, CIO, a VP of recruiting, and a VP of business development. They meet weekly without her. The weekly meetings are action-oriented, looking at where the customers are and what the numbers are saying. Then they come together for a monthly meeting with Mona, to examine the challenges the business is facing, and quarterly, for more strategic reviews. Business is booming now, so everyone is running very fast. The company has other offices, in North Carolina, Connecticut, Indiana, and New York. Without Mona there much of the time, how does it all hang together?

"We all have SMART goals," said Mona. "SMART stands for smart, measurable, achievable, realistic, and timely. We come up with them together. There are many dependencies in this business, so we have to come up with goals as a team and help one another achieve them. Everyone is accountable for his own, but it's important for everybody to know what everyone else is trying to achieve. They are accountable to one another."

When I talked to Mike McBrierty, Mona's VP of recruiting, I could see why she said he was a rock. His is an industry that has become notorious for over-promising and under-delivering, but Mike comes across as a laid-back, laconic kind of guy, which is unexpected in such an aggressive labor market. You don't get the feeling that he is easily swayed by anyone or anything.

"We have one of the lowest turnover rates in the industry—in an industry that's known for turnover. But we have really great assignments and that tends to keep really great people. Plus, Mona's pretty sensitive to other people. She has a young and growing family herself. She knows what it's like and she's empathetic to what other people go through."

Mike's job is to hire and manage the company's recruiters. If Eliassen doesn't have the best recruiters, they won't have the best consultants, and the sales team won't succeed. On the other hand, the recruiters are dependent on business development to generate the projects that keep their consultants busy. Mike's SMART goals reveal these dependencies. Among other things, he must find trainees and develop recruiters internally. He has to develop a strategy for marketing to the recruiters that he wishes to attract to Eliassen. He has to ensure that he is hiring fast enough but not too fast. At the same time, he works on building up leadership within his own recruiting team as well as improving the crossover between recruiting and sales. As security becomes a bigger issue in the software world, he also needs to ensure that his recruiting team has the expertise needed to satisfy that emerging market.

"We are all encouraged to challenge ourselves. We do SMART goals at the beginning of the year, monitor them quarterly, and reset them mid-year. Do they work? I think they do. They're a challenge, that's for sure. They stretch us and test us, and sometimes we take on too many. But if there's a SMART goal we're not getting to, that impacts the business. They work because we can all see that they drive the activity in the business."

Mike keeps his goals posted on the board next to him. That means he can see them all the time, and so can his colleagues.

This kind of transparency isn't just cosmetic. It reveals one of the biggest but unsung successes at the Eliassen Group: the elimination of politics.

"The leadership team used to be political, but it's not today. We've learned to identify the issue, solve the issue, and leave the room with relationships intact. We focus on the issue, not the person. It's hard to get to that point and it is uncomfortable, but overall, at the end, you feel better."

This is so unusual that at first I didn't believe it. Every company has politics. In small businesses the politics are often more intense because everything is so personal and there's nowhere to hide. But everyone I talked to in the Eliassen Group told the same story, of meetings where the focus was on issues and not on personalities.

"We get along well enough," said head of sales Peggy Murphy, "but we're not shy about confronting one another. When I first joined the leadership team, I thought, "Yikes, these people really tell it like it is!" But now it doesn't faze me. You get very constructive feedback. We call it care-frontational. It happens on a daily basis and is pretty normal. People new to the group are kind of amazed. They'll say, "Do you really say those things to each other?" But it's all a way of being more productive and healthier."

In other words, Eliassen Group has achieved something most companies aim for but few achieve: honesty. Not jockeying for position, not posturing, but honesty. Key to this achievement is a decision that Mona made that provides real insight into her leadership style. She does not chair the monthly and quarterly meetings. She gets an outsider to do it. In this way she is not the focus of attention. People don't position themselves for her approval because she isn't running the meeting. Instead, the meetings are run by Ken Dreyer, who started as Mona's coach and now works for the company as a facilitator. The meetings are therefore run by someone who has no power to make decisions. It is as far from a command-and-control management style as it's possible to get.

"Ken is active in the leadership team, and he is an unbelievable person," said Peggy Murphy. "I don't know whether he keeps us in check or we keep ourselves in check, but we all do whatever we need to do."

Mike McBrierty shared her enthusiasm: "Ken's very good at keeping things in perspective. He has an independent view and can look at things objectively. He thinks of questions that we don't. It's very common for companies to be political, but we've gotten to the point where we don't b--- s--- one another. We just call it out."

The success of Mona's team owes a lot to the trust she has placed in it and the structures she has devised to bring focus and honesty to her business.

"Mona gets involved as much as she can, but she also lets us do as much as we can. She cares about everyone in the company, and she knows everyone very well. Everyone feels that she's available and approachable," said Dave McKeen. He is in charge of the company's finances, but he's not your typical accounting guy. He is more passionate and more enthusiastic, and it's clear that he loves the freedom he has found at Eliassen.

"We can challenge Mona about the direction of the company, and she's good with that. Just the other day, when I was very involved looking at M&A opportunities for us, someone asked her when she would look to sell. She said she'd look at any offer that was made but that ultimately it was up to the leadership team. And she owns 100 percent of the company!"

When Mona delegates, she means it. She lets other people run her meetings; she lets them run the business. No one should mistake this for abdication. She may not be around all the time, but she knows what's going on, in detail. She may not make most of the decisions, but she's always reviewing them. In fact, she provides a high caliber of oversight and review that is only possible because she isn't embroiled in the day-to-day. It is a powerful combination of detail and vision that it would be a mistake to underestimate.

"The prior president," recalled Dave, "he kind of assumed she couldn't handle too much detail. Gosh, was he wrong! For instance, she and I were talking about some numbers, and she caught me on something—she had been doing all the numbers in her head! She's financially literate, so she makes it easy for me to communicate with her. She knows exactly what I'm talking about. She also has a great memory. We challenge each other on accuracy, and she often gets the best of me. It's not that I feel I report to her but that I work with her."

"The thing is," reflected Peggy Murphy, "the first time I saw how she mixed with everyone, how down-to-earth she was, that got to me. She had been incredibly successful at a young age, but she doesn't take herself too seriously. She could be full of herself, but she isn't. Anybody can call Mona or stop in her office. She's a pretty unique person."

It is not about control. Mona is powerful because she gives power to people who can handle it and who have the resources they need to manage it. Her leadership is not one of domination, achieved by being the smartest, toughest, and longest-working overachiever in the room. She leads by orchestration. By putting the right people in the right place. By intervening when she needs to and leaving things alone when she can. Her presence hovers over the office when she's not there. Her values and ambitions for the company reside inside everyone's head.

Orchestration is a female form of leadership. This doesn't mean that every female business owner runs things this way or that it is the only way women lead. It seems to be both a very comfortable and an immensely effective way for women to run their businesses.

Lauri Union's world of steel manufacturing is a far cry from Boston high-tech. Based in Fayetteville, North Carolina, the Union Corrugating Company was a family business. Started by Lauri's grandfather after World War II, it began to lose money and customers when her father, who didn't want to run it, handed over the management to two outsiders. In 1990, Lauri, a freshly minted Harvard MBA, took over the day-to-day running of the business—or almost. Her fiancé lived in Boston, and neither of them wanted to move to North Carolina. So Lauri commuted.

"At first, in 1992, I was there every day. I'd leave Boston every Sunday and fly home on Friday. But after about a year or so, I started to taper off until I was there only two days a week. By 2002 I went to the company probably four days a month." By 2002 she was also expecting her second child.

Lauri's decision not to base herself at the company's head-quarters was pretty audacious. Had she been an employee instead of an owner, it seems unlikely that anyone would have believed it could work. But it did work, triumphantly. When she took over the business, sales were in a slump, and the company had recently lost its business with Lowe's, a major outlet for their cor-rugated metal panels. Customer service was appalling, and long-time customers were wondering why they should continue to use a company that had many cheaper competitors. Over a period of ten years Lauri changed all that. She introduced new products, revamped the sales team, and rebuilt the company's reputation. Reversing the decline she had inherited, Lauri saw the company begin to grow again.[2] And most of the time, she wasn't even there.

"We used to joke that the less I was there, the better the company did. It was true!" she said with a laugh.

Was it true?

"Well, we had nine manufacturing plants, and the company headquarters was attached to one of them. There was always the danger that what I heard from that plant was out of proportion because I happened to be there. Being remote gave me a more balanced picture of the whole company. Also, having an open-door policy could have meant that I'd get sucked into stuff others could handle. The fact that I was not there made the management team stronger because they weren't dependent on me. The company's growth was not held back by the limits of what I could do."

The company's growth was not held back by the limits of what I could do: What a remarkable comment from the successful leader of a turnaround. So, if Lauri wasn't holding anyone back, what was she doing?

"I focused on three key things: customer relationships, the company's reputation, and openness in our employee relationships. People who were not trusted were asked to leave. We had to have a company where everyone could trust everyone else. Hiring was never solely about skills but also about cultural fit. People joined because they liked the values, and that's how they got embedded. So I just had to nurture it."

Not being there every day also meant that the company had to develop a great deal of discipline in its operations. "A lot of our competitors," recalled Lauri, "let all their plants run autonomously, but that meant you couldn't really see where the problems were. What we did was institute best practices: If something worked really well in one plant, we rolled it out everywhere. That way we shared the best innovations and could spot where the problems were. I couldn't be going around to them all the time, but I could always see what was happening."

Moreover, not being on-site every day gave Lauri time to think, which is often the hardest thing for CEOs to make time for. Research shows that women tend to reflect more, considering options and outcomes more broadly before making decisions.[3] They are very comfortable making those decisions, but they prefer to think about them and gain more information about them before making irrevocable choices. Sometimes being at a distance from operations allows the time for the quiet that such reflection requires.

Ten years later the company is doing well and has a compounded growth rate of 20 percent and even faster growth in its profitability. During a time of turmoil and shortages in the steel industry, Union Corrugating was able to retrieve its contract with Lowes, open new facilities, and gain market share. "We have weathered those storms better than our competitors," said Lauri modestly. And all by not being there.

The nature of her business means that Lauri will never run a virtual company. Even in the new economy, manufacturing needs people and materials in the same place. But a services business doesn't have the same requirements. When Paige Arnof-Fenn started Mavens & Moguls, she knew that her business would have to be virtual; there was no way she'd ever get the talent she wanted under one roof. Forty marketing mavens and moguls were available to work on brand strategies, new product development, market research, and marketing strategies. Some already had consulting clients and saw this as a way to get more work; others simply liked the prospect of working together. There is no Mavens & Moguls headquarters. There is just Paige and her cell phone.

"It didn't dawn on me that it wouldn't work, but I didn't expect it to take off as fast and to scale as consistently as it has. I think it was the right idea at the right time, and also I have the right connections to make it work."

The word *connections* is crucial to Paige's business because she is the connector. It is Paige who holds the business together, finds new business, pulls teams together, and reassigns them when they're done. So who's in charge?

"That's a good question. I guess ultimately it's me, but because everyone in the group is someone I respect and admire, I almost never make a decision in a vacuum. How much we will charge, the scope and timing of a project—the team has to agree on that. We've had a few situations where I sensed a client was not someone we wanted to continue with long term, but even that is ultimately up to the team. If the team is willing to put up with the attitude for the money, we'll stay with it. I guess the only decision I make alone is what day we run the payroll."

Paige laughs heartily at this rather scrawny vision of executive power. It would be wrong to say, however, that she's not interested in power. If power is the ability to get things done, it's hard to find anyone more passionate about that than Paige. But her focus is on the business, not herself.

"There are no politics in this business. What stuns me is how much time in conventional companies is wasted in meetings and useless squabbling. I feel as though I spend almost all my days on things that really matter and so little on face time or posturing. I was decent at that stuff when I worked on Wall Street and at Procter & Gamble, but I hated spending so much time on it. Time is the most precious thing you have, and you don't want to waste it on politics."

One of the mavens referred to Paige as the "center spoke," paying tribute to the time and effort that Paige put in to pull everyone together.[4] Once she does that, she lets the teams do the work.

"I'm well suited to it. It plays to my strengths," Paige commented. "You can never get lazy or complacent. My standards are high, and our clients expect everyone to be rock stars. To keep people motivated I have to always be on. I am a little compulsive, but I always want to hit the ball out of the park every day, every time—even if the client is happy getting to second base. It helps to have a sense of humor and not need too much sleep, which I really don't.

"In existing corporations," she said, "you inherit colleagues and hierarchies. Here, we choose what we do and how we do it. If there is something we don't like, I can fix it immediately. I don't want it to brew. I cut it out and move on. When I was at Procter & Gamble, I used to say, 'If I could do this *my* way . . .' Well, now I do get to do it my way. And we keep doubling every year!"

"Almost everyone agrees that the command-and-control corporate model will not carry us into the twenty-first century. It is no longer possible to figure it out from the top," wrote Peter Senge nearly ten years ago.[5] Leaders such as Mona Eliassen, Lauri Union, and Paige Arnof-Fenn seem to know this instinctively. They're uncomfortable with hierarchies in part because they're modest. It doesn't feel very feminine to stand atop their employees and proclaim omniscience, and it doesn't feel very smart, either. By making their egos less of a force inside the company, these CEOs make space for others' intelligence and creativity. They unleash the potential of many instead of focusing on the power of the one. And in doing this, they (perhaps unwittingly) remove some of the power struggles from within the company. After all, if the model is collegiate, fighting to become top dog becomes irrelevant.

This may sound easy, but it isn't. It is hard to think of any single area of Mona's or Paige's business that either woman couldn't handle brilliantly herself. They don't do so because they know the greater power of empowering others. Lauri Union used to see customers herself. She doesn't have to do that anymore because she has people in place whom she can trust and who share her values. This doesn't mean that it isn't hard sometimes not to intervene.

"I know just about everything there is to know about mission statements," pronounced Geraldine Laybourne, CEO of Oxygen Media. "I've done them for years." Of course she has. Having led the creation of *Nickelodeon, Nick at Night,* and the *Rugrats,* there's next to nothing that Laybourne doesn't know about market positioning. "It would have been the easiest thing in the world for me to sit down and write a mission statement."

Laybourne can justly claim to have raised more investment for her business than any other woman alive—some $500 million. Oxygen launched with enormous fanfare, and she was named the twentieth most powerful woman in American business by *Fortune* magazine. But when she needed a mission statement, her business was, in her own words, "a lot of mess"—and a lot of public mess. The business had been trying to do too many things at once on the Internet and on cable. It had big layoffs as the Internet group was disbanded. The company faced public skepticism and even derision. It urgently needed focus and tight definition. If it was to turn itself around, everyone who worked there needed to be able to make quick decisions based on a crystal clear—and shared—idea of what the company stood for. How tempting it must have been, therefore, to just sit down, hammer out the mission statement fast, and get moving.

"But that isn't what I did. I put the general counsel in charge of drawing up the mission statement. He is the fairest person I know—and he has patience. He involved everyone in the process. Everyone here was able to make a contribution, everyone here was listened to and everyone became part of the process."

Geraldine believes in leadership as orchestration, but that doesn't make it easy for her.

"At times my tongue was bloody, I had to bite it so often! I had to sit in on so many meetings and just keep quiet! But at the end everyone was invested in it. After all, if I could hold my tongue, that said a lot for the process. I didn't have to control it. It was painful for me. I wanted to pitch in! But they came up with something that was better than anything I could have done."[6]

The new Oxygen is much stronger than before. Viewers are up, awareness is up, and the company has outperformed its own business plan for several years running. It has just exceeded fifty million subscribers, a magic number in the cable business when multiples really start to kick in. There are many explanations for the turnaround, and the fact that everyone knows what they're doing and why is surely one of them.

Leadership, in the way that women such as Mona Eliassen and Geraldine Laybourne practice it, is not about vast amounts of self-promotion or magazine covers, and it is not about being the smartest person in the room. It isn't about control or issuing orders. It is about unleashing the ability of others.

Every time I've asked to meet with a female business leader, I've been struck by two things. First, they all ask why I am interested in them. They don't see that they, or what they are doing, merits attention. Second, when I meet them, they always make a point of introducing me to their management teams and sometimes to the whole company. I haven't requested those introductions; they just happen. These leaders understand and demonstrate that the team is responsible for the company's success. Such women are the conductors, but they know that without the orchestra there is no music.

This is strikingly at odds with popular notions of leadership.[7] It bears little or no relation to the leadership style of military generals, presidents, or the magazine cover CEOs who appear to be the single shining light of their organizations. (No male CEO has ever questioned why I wanted to interview him.) Nor is it part of the macho fight for top spot. It is about the much harder task of finding the right people and teaching them—by coaching, by goal setting, and by example—how to collaborate effectively.

I recall a time in my own career when, along with my fellow CEOs, I was asked to present the core products and promise of my company. When I made the presentation alongside my senior software architect, I was roundly criticized; I was told it looked as though I wasn't competent to speak for myself. Years later I sat through a company presentation of a Fortune 500 company where all the divisional heads but one were male. Only the lone female included in her presentation the names of all her team leaders. When I pointed this out to the CEO, he mistook my meaning and apologized for her. "She is no good at self-promotion," he said.

But her kind of leadership wasn't weakness. It represented a recognition (conscious or otherwise) that excellence in the modern economy can no longer be about solo acts. These women aren't achieving excellence through internal competition and shoot-outs but through collaboration. They aren't ranking people; they're nurturing them. This is not an easy option, and it can be especially painful when the money in play is your own.

"It's scary," said Brenda Rivers of Andavo Travel. "It's scary because you have to hand over control, and it's *your money*! I had to do it because it's part of my philosophy and also because I didn't know a lot about the travel business. I have no idea how to book an airline ticket, and I can't tell you what all those symbols mean. I make fun of myself, but that's their expertise, not mine. I hired people who knew more than I did, and I think that's the right thing to do."

Brenda, Geraldine, and Mona are all what Jim Collins, in *Good to Great,* would describe as "Level 5 leaders." They aren't just competent. They aren't just effective. With a weird mixture of humility and personal will, they nurture their teams to greatness. That's how Andavo survived 9/11. It's how Geraldine and Mona survived the tech bust. These are strong women who don't need to show off their brilliance.

"It's like kayaking," said Brenda. "Servant leader, that's me. I lead from behind, and I hold the rudder. I make sure everyone is fit, encouraged, and enthused, and knows that we will get through."

Leadership of this kind isn't great only in a crisis. Because creativity in our age is rarely about the individual working alone to construct a brilliant new product, it lies at the heart of contemporary innovation. "In fields of complex, modern business, we are clearly in an era where the ideas of a single person seldom lead to significant progress," said Alex Broer, former director of research at IBM.[8] Instead, innovation is driven by being able to talk to people, creating the conditions in which they tell the truth, and giving them the courage to follow through on their ideas.

June Coldren is a bubbly Yankee lawyer from Pennsylvania, which means she is the antithesis of everything you'd expect from the chief executive of an oil company working in the Gulf of Mexico. Everything June has learned she's learned the hard way— by doing it. She has persisted and succeeded very much on her own terms.

"You have to understand being a woman and being a woman in an oil field. The industry is such a good ol' boy industry, such a man's world. You have oil and gas *and* the South! I was shocked at first to see how different it is from the North. I feel women are treated in a different way down here. We aren't supposed to be leaders and running our own companies, so there can be problems. For example, when I call to invite people to lunch, one of my clients might say, "Well, I'd love to, but my wife won't let me have lunch with just you." And it's just a business lunch!

"In my business, many companies who are trying to get contracts will hire ex-strippers as salespeople. It is truly amazing. They come in their Lucite high heels! I can't imagine that they know anything about what they're selling. Well, we don't do that. Our salespeople are appropriately dressed and know what they are talking about. We are out there to get business and give good service, and that's it."

As a "foreigner" working in an industry where there aren't many women, June Coldren could have tried to fit in, to work the way her competitor companies did, but she didn't. She hasn't used sex to sell, and she hasn't used machismo to succeed. In fact, staying true to her naturally collaborative style is what enabled her to identify an innovative business opportunity.

Cenergy's core business involves providing contractors to work on oil rigs. The oil companies don't want to employ them directly, so Cenergy employs them and hires them out to client companies such as Chevron Texaco. It is a cyclical business, and at any one time June may have a hundred or more people on her books. Watching how all the oil and gas companies work gave her a unique insight into the industry, and that insight led to June's second company, Cenergy Logistics.

"The companies in the Gulf all have platforms and rigs within five hundred feet of one another, but they all use their own helicopters and their own boats to transport people and materials. It's incredibly wasteful. So I thought: If we could all publish the schedules of when the boats and helicopters were going out there, we could pool those resources and everyone would save a stack of money. So we built a logistics business that does just that. You can go onto the Web site, see where there are empty seats, drag and drop and make your reservation. You can do the same with boats that are bringing fluid, mud, people, water, groceries— anything. The Web site shows you how much space is available and you can just book it up.

"Many companies were afraid to publish this stuff; they thought it was proprietary. But I argued that if they were more open, they'd save so much money. When they see how much they're wasting, it really changes their minds! There has been some resistance to sharing, just part of the good ol' boy syndrome; you know, a guy wants his helicopter, and he wants it now! It's up to my company to say, "You have to wait two hours for a scheduled flight." Gradually, the companies are becoming cooperative. It's good for the environment, and they save so much money!

"Could a guy have done this? My logisticians are all men. The company that developed it, in India, was all men. But it takes a woman's brain to see it, implement it, and sell it. It was less threatening to them. I could see past the individual companies and all their pride, which was costing them so much, and work with them."

It is very hard to see this kind of leadership because it is almost invisible. It isn't chest-thumping, it isn't loud, and it isn't about being the expert. At Delaire, CEO Lori Hallock is the least educated member of her team. Delaire is a technology company—and Lori isn't technical.

"Without a technology degree, you can be a technology company if you can tap into the people you need to solve the problem. I've been fortunate to have those people close to me. We have a very resourceful team here, very determined, and we all help one another out."

When I met with Lori's team, it was obvious that she had a couple of technology superstars working for her. It wasn't obvious because she said so, or because they said so. It was obvious from the work they had done for customers such as Lucent and Cisco. But everyone on this team carries their learning lightly. They tease one another a lot. They're self-deprecating. Building this quality of camaraderie has taken a great deal of time and honesty. Jim Farina, Delaire's CTO, said he has worked in places that were bigger and just as open and honest, but "it is different here. The men are different. The men here can work for a woman. We've had guys who couldn't. Just had tremendous egos. Thought they were running the show. It caused a lot of tension and a lot of distraction."

This orchestrated style of leadership has immense consequences for companies. That is obvious when you watch how the management teams operate, how they talk and feel about one another. In small companies where political tensions can be intense, being liberated from them carries immense value. Being able to hire smart people and allow them to get even smarter is clearly a business advantage. But we've seen leadership fads come and go. One day leaders are teachers; the next day what matters is that they are authentic. Is this kind of leadership anything more than just another passing phase?

I think the "servant leader" (as Brenda Rivers described it) matters because of the nature of the current business world. Perhaps there was a time when it was possible for a leader to know enough to call all the shots and when expertise was all that was required to establish and execute on a clear vision. I'm not even sure that that time was so long ago. What is obvious is that it's now gone. The forces operating on any single company are now too numerous, too complex, and too fast moving for any individual leader to master. The demand for innovation is too insistent. It is no longer possible for a single individual to know enough, so leadership becomes about building functional teams that can. It is about harnessing what James Surowiecki would call the wisdom of crowds.[9]

The wisdom of crowds works like this: Groups of people working together make better decisions than single individuals—but that delivers diversity only if the individuals in the group are different, are allowed to remain different, and are allowed to be honest. Creating an environment in which people can be honest requires that leadership not be intimidating; otherwise, everyone just tries to second-guess the leader, and the value of the group's differences is lost. Servant leadership understands that the way to extract value from teams is not passive, it isn't about getting out of the way. It is by regularly encouraging, rewarding, and promoting the key values—honesty, openness, learning, and debate—that you make groups smarter, more creative, and more innovative.

Many claim that our "female" qualities hold us back inside large traditional corporations. We are not dominant enough, we are too collaborative, and we aren't very comfortable singing our own praises or pushing ourselves to the front. Such behaviors are ostensibly bad for business, and they are often offered as an excuse for women's failure to reach the top. I would argue that, far from being a problem, such behaviors represent a solution because when we run our own businesses, where ownership already bestows power and where we can more easily determine the values of our companies, these same characteristics turn out to be tremendously advantageous. We are *not* dominant, which means that we aren't threatened when our employees know more than we do. We *are* collaborative and understand that part of being collaborative is knowing when to bite our lips. By not singing our own praises, we leave space for more than one hero in every company. By not hogging the spotlight, we let whole teams shine.

Only an idiot would mistake this for weakness.

7. Customer Love

Basically, we have a policy that says: "If you have any problems (health issues or child care issues), we will try to work around them until you're ready to come back. We will make compromises in order to keep people."

That policy is the bedrock of the employee policies at the Union Corrugating Company. Instead of playing the heavy, instead of asserting her dominance over them, CEO Lauri Union wants to help her people over their difficulties until they come back to work. People come first.

This attitude makes a difference to Union's employees, but it doesn't stop there. Once you decide you want to work with people instead of trying to dominate them, it changes every relationship you touch. The culture you build for employees is the culture experienced by customers. They become mirror images of each other. Union Corrugating's desire to work with its employees is the same as its commitment to work with its customers.

It hasn't always been that way. When Lauri Union decided to take over the family business, she knew its problems, having studied them as part of her Harvard MBA. One of the key systemic issues Lauri confronted immediately was her company's attitude to customers. Few orders were shipped on time. Many goods were defective. When customers complained, they were told either that it was their own fault or that there was nothing the company could do about it. Despite operating in a fiercely competitive market, there was little that the company did to make their customers love them.

When Lauri started as president, she noticed that UCC's management talked about their customers as if they were one big nuisance. Foremen refused to deliver anything until they had a full delivery truck. They complained when customers didn't send in orders efficiently but often placed several small orders a week rather than one big one. And if goods were late, faulty, or incomplete, as seemed to happen with monotonous regularity, the customers had the gall to complain. In other words, the company had developed a culture that hated its customers. This is not nearly as uncommon as you might think.

Lauri had the same attitude toward her customers as she did toward her employees: We want to work *with* you. We want to accommodate you. We are in this together. And she succeeded—not just in keeping some of her old and valued customers but eventually in winning back business from Lowe's.

Harvard's Shoshana Zuboff, in her analysis of twentieth-century managerial structures, makes the argument that the old way of doing business was built by men who took a male concept of power (domination) and built corporate structures that served it (the pyramidal hierarchy).[1] They kept as far away as possible from customers because most customers were women. Managerial men, said Zuboff, did not want to be seen serving in public those whom they dominated in private. For them, service was a dirty word.

But for Lauri Union and many women like her, quite the opposite is true. Service is ennobling. Whereas her predecessors derided their customers, Lauri believed them—and wanted to serve them well. Where they put their own interests first (the efficient deployment of delivery trucks), she put her customers' interests first. And it helped her save the company.

It is no coincidence that the culture of respecting employees' needs, which Lauri espoused, was echoed by the respect for customers' needs that Lauri needed to inspire. They are two faces of a single coin. Both demonstrate empathy, humility, and a pronounced lack of ego. It is the exact opposite of corporate narcissism, the trait that lets one see only from the company's perspective. When companies treat their employees with respect, they create the conditions in which those same employees can and will treat their customers with respect. You can't have one without the other. And so culture doesn't just deliver better employees who do better work for longer—it also inspires a healthier attitude toward customers.

At National Van Lines, treating drivers with respect is critical; it may be the only way the company has of communicating its values. Customers may never see anyone from National, but they interact with the drivers. So the drivers hold the company's reputation in their hands.

"Bear in mind," said Maureen Beal, "that we're often dealing with customers at a very emotional time in their lives. It's the third most stressful event in your life—after bereavement and divorce! And the most important person in a move is the driver. He can make or break the move."

"Like Lon," she remembered. "Lon won a lot of praise when he was moving a man with senile dementia. This elderly gentleman was leaving his home where he'd lived forever, and it was a very emotional time for him and his daughter. This old man was really fascinated by Lon's truck, so Lon let him ride in the cab and drove him around the neighborhood. He just loved it. We got a letter later from his daughter saying what a big difference that had made to her and to her dad."

As you would expect from a CEO who remembers stories like that, winning customers' love is deeply woven into the company's processes. After their move, all customers receive a survey along with a personal letter from Maureen in which she thanks them for their business and says she will personally review the results of the survey (which she does). There are several good reasons to return the surveys—prize drawings and the chance to win various gifts. Remarkably, especially when considering the exhaustion that follows any move, they get a 12 percent return rate.

"The one thing we were all startled by was how many were so positive because we were used to being reactionary—people usually only write in if they have something to complain about. Our claims department never used to see anything that wasn't a claim, and now they're hearing from people they want to adopt and take home to their mom!

"I look at every single survey," said Maureen, "and it's really striking how many are good now. It has really changed. When we have a dissatisfied customer, Jorja calls them at once. That they get called by a vice president shows we are paying attention. And she fixes it."

"It really counts, being able to respond to a customer honestly and say: This is an exception," said Jorja. "Sometimes we have excellent drivers and something goes wrong. And sometimes we find out it wasn't the driver's problem. We go to great lengths to be fair to everyone. It permeates our whole methodology. Maureen won't have a policy that isn't fair and customer focused."

Drivers are graded according to the surveys. The four-star and five-star drivers get paid more. Drivers who seem to be having problems come in for more training. Problems get fixed fast. And customers know that they are heard, that they come first. If anyone working for National Van Lines thought service was demeaning, they wouldn't last long.

A large component of any van line's business comes from the military, who are endlessly relocating their personnel. Unlike single individuals who, once moved, may never move again, the military is a long-term customer whose satisfaction can make a big impact on the bottom line and on the way the company feels about itself.

"Our military business," said Maureen, "is probably a higher percentage of our work than it is for most other lines. In fact, just the other day I had one of my shining moments. There is a general who just retired from logistics. His daughter was moving from Texas to Colorado, and he told his daughter to use us. I happened to be in Texas the day of her move, so I stopped by. I was so touched by his recommendation, and I was so glad I could drop in. It is things like that that make this job a dream."

Of course it helps to like people, to empathize with them, and to be able to identify with their needs. Like employees, most customers aren't malevolent; they just want to be treated with respect and fairness.

"I believe in treating people as I would like to be treated," said Linda Prince. She is the receptionist at Otis Technology, and as well as welcoming visitors to the company, she also answers the customer support line—so customers get to talk to a human being.

"I like talking to people," she said, and went on to prove it.

"I know how it feels when something isn't what you expected or when it doesn't work. At one point we started getting a lot of complaints that the patch (this tiny piece of cloth) kept getting trapped in the barrel. So I told Doreen, and they redesigned it. And when they'd done that, I went back to my records. I'd saved all the e-mails and made notes of all the phone calls, and I contacted all those customers to tell them about the redesign and to let them know that I was sending them some of the new ones. Only one person didn't say it was perfect!"

At Otis any customer complaint that can't be instantly resolved goes straight to the CEO's office. Doreen finds that most of the time the problem is that the instructions haven't been properly understood, but that doesn't mean she blames the customer. She blames the instruction leaflet and makes sure that the next time it is clearer. At Linda's reception desk is a thick folder filled with letters from soldiers thanking Otis for their products and their service. It is a lot bigger than her file of complaints.

"The key thing is to remember that the customer is a different person," said Peggy Murphy at the Eliassen Group. She understands that her job in sales is not to talk about herself and her company but to listen to her customers' needs and to build a relationship.

"You have to make a connection with that person by finding out where they vacation or how many kids they have. It is your job to find it. It is not to tell them all they never wanted to know about the Eliassen Group. Your job is to find out about *them*. Don't just go in and try to sell them something. Don't kiss on the first date. Get to know them. Build trust and figure out if we really can help them or not."

Peggy is very clear that she doesn't want a short-term relationship with her customers. She will invest time in her relationships because she knows that it will build more long-term business from a satisfied client. She knows that all business is relationships, and relationships take time.

"It's not rocket science. You have to be yourself and try to solve their problems. But you have to remember: It's about *them,* not you."

"If the client is frustrated," said Pat Loret de Mola, "I ask myself: What are we doing wrong? We are young and humble enough to use this for introspection. Companies can become very arrogant as they grow and become more established. So an issue for us will be: Can we stay humble? It's a high-quality problem to have."

Pat has spent most of her life working in high-powered positions on Wall Street. How does she come to understand and embrace humility? "It's common sense. It's really just about people, about relationships. We are always trying to know the people that use our system better and better so that there's more of a bond. It makes for better business. High-tech with high touch. In some ways I think the higher the tech, the more touch there has to be. And the better we know our customers, the better we get as a business. They keep us on the ball."

It's a story Joni Walton at Danlee Medical Supplies knows well. Her business does not compete on price, she said. It wins and keeps customers by providing outstanding service. The company maintains high margins because their customers love the service they receive.

"Customers call and ask us for all kinds of things, and our answer is always yes. A mental institution called and asked if we could supply them with disposable scrubs. Apparently, some of their patients come in against their will; they're all messed up and have nothing to wear. So we created an entire line of disposable scrubs for them. Who knew that market was even there?

"Our customers always work in a very busy environment, and they expect us to bend over backward for them. That's why we've been successful—because we go the extra mile. We will never have voice mail. When you are a customer and you have a problem, you want it fixed now. So people call and get a human being. They are never told 'I'll get back to you.' We fix their problems right away."

Joni is particularly sensitive to the current fashion for making the customer do all the work. "Wherever I go, I'm critiquing everyone. The other day I was at a swimming pool supply place, and this woman and I were talking about how everything is self-service these days. All this little old lady wanted was for someone to help her carry this huge gallon of chlorine to the car. The manager said he'd send someone out to help her, but of course he never did. I ended up carrying it to the car for her. It was just awful the way that the supply place had completely given up on the idea of service.

"I think you should never make it painful for the customer. All these companies ask if you have your account number, product code, and price code. All the work is pushed down to the customer! We don't do business that way. We have personal relationships with them, and when they call up, we say, 'Oh, if you're ordering that, did you know we had such-and-such a product that goes with it?' It's thinking about what they need, not what we need. If you can't find some information, just write down what they want and figure it out once they're off the phone. Don't waste their time doing your work."

It is clear that Joni takes a lot of pride delivering this quality of service. Like any company, Danlee has its fair share of high-maintenance customers. Joni's approach to them is not to blame them or try to alter their behavior. She is on a permanent mission to win them over.

"One of our most difficult customers negotiates *everything*. And everyone lives in fear of picking up one of her calls. One day she called and gave everyone a hard time. Then she asked for me, and I was thinking, 'Oh, no.' And she said, 'Joni, I just wanted to tell you how friendly and helpful everyone in your company is. How do you find them, and how do you keep them?' She took the time to tell me that!"

Joni can empathize with her customers; she knows they are as busy and stressed as she often is herself. She wants to alleviate not exacerbate that. She does not want to contribute to what Shoshana Zuboff calls "the chasm of rage and despair" that typically separates customers from businesses. She knows that doing a good job is more satisfying than doing a mediocre one, and she also knows that it makes her business more valuable.

"We compete on service, and no one can beat us at that. We get customers and keep them because of the quality of service we provide. We even get customers sending us little cards and notes thanking us—can you imagine? And that makes my company more valuable."

Joni sees service as a source of pride and of profit. As she found in the case of disposable scrubs, companies that learn to listen well end up letting their customers design their products. In Denver, Open Scan's John Franco has devoted a good part of his life to understanding the trouble his customers have when electronic payments go wrong—exception mail. Franco knows that normal payment processing costs his customers only about eleven cents per payment, but the exceptions cost anywhere from $2 to $6 to fix manually and they take longer. If he can automate fixing those mistakes, his customers get more money, faster, and at a lower cost.

"I spend day and night thinking about dirty mail," said John. "People put the wrong data all over the place—so we wrote a module to figure that out. It'll handle 400,000 bizarre pieces of information with an accuracy rate of 96 percent now. Sometimes we just guessed that what we saw happening in one customer location was probably happening everywhere else, and we were right: It was happening everywhere else. People were making mistakes everywhere, so basically we designed the whole thing from the ground up with our customers—just watching where they were hurting."

As chief technology officers go, John Franco is more interested in other people and their problems than any I've ever seen. He isn't inventing cool stuff and then trying to force it on customers. He's listening, hard.

"I try to stay close to tech support and testing so I hear every single complaint about the software and everything we've done well—and I get a lot of ideas from that. I want to do what customers want next. There is so much! I have a whole list of things to improve: accuracy, decreasing the amount of manual involvement, speeding up the whole system. With every customer, I try to find a way to improve a piece and still deliver the product on time."

Nadine is visibly proud of what John has produced. She herself is every inch the saleswoman, chomping Twizzlers all day and constantly thinking about how, with John, they can make the Open Scan software more productive and also easier to use.

"John has taken what I created to another level. He figured out how to simplify it, not just the software but everything—even the training manual. It's only one page now! People don't want to read hundreds of pages; they want to get the software installed and get going."

"People like working with Nadine," said John Heap. He works for APEX, which makes the scanners on which Open Scan's software runs. They've partnered for a long time and have overseen many customer installations together.

"Nadine really understands customers. In this type of marketplace there are always little things that customers need, and if you can't do it or won't do it, you don't have a chance at the business. Plenty of companies out there will promise you anything, but they can't do it. That's not Nadine. Every time Nadine says she will do something, it happens. It isn't just because she's the CEO; it's because she really understands her customers—and half the time she's ahead of them. She understands their problem better than they do!"

Without any investment in her company and with a small team and marketing budget, Nadine can sell her technology to Fortune 500 companies because she and everyone at Open Scan listen well. They have let the customers design the product because they know that's how to build something that their customers want, need, and value.

"Of course you love your customers," said Nadine. "You have to love your customers. Everything in a business is an expense except them!"

She'd find a soul mate in New Jersey where Lori Hallock's Delaire Inc. displays customer satisfaction charts in the middle of the assembly areas. Lori attributes the company's very survival to the ability to win and retain immensely loyal customers.

"When the telecoms boom died," she recalled, "there was a big influx of talented engineers. We had customers coming to us looking for solutions, and we could tap into our extended network to find the right talent. We had the customers. We had to respond fast, but we were supplying systems then, not just components, because we could react so quickly. Cisco, Alcatel, and Agilent were all asking if we could provide solutions that no one else could come up with. We were getting these requests worldwide. Customers come to us now. They know we'll listen and we'll work fast for them."

Delaire recently won a Silver Gull award for economic development, a fancy way of saying they stayed in business through tough times and kept jobs and business in New Jersey. But for Lori the real reward is seeing her business thrive. Halfway through 2005 her revenue had already surpassed the total revenue for the preceding year.

Simon Huizer made some of the company's first fiber-optic cable, but cable is a low-margin commoditized business, so he's delighted to see Delaire winning more and more valuable contracts.

"When we were making cable, lots of people were making cable—and lots of it was really poor quality. But we wouldn't put our name on it if it wasn't good. We'd do 100 percent testing and pass 100 percent. The thing about cables is that they are the last thing ordered and the first thing needed, so they're always a rush job. But that's no reason to do them poorly. Now I think we have a really good reputation because we were always so careful. People know we supply quality work."

"Our customers trust us with some of their toughest problems," said Lori. "And that's great because that's where we can make a big impact: getting hard problems to solve that those businesses really value. They trust us because Simon and Jim really listen. They don't just build what the customers ask for. They work hard to understand the basic problem and to figure out the best possible solution to it even if that turns out to be something the customer never imagined."

Jim Farina, the chief technologist, has a professorial air. He has worked in technology companies large and small, and he gives the impression that there's very little he hasn't seen.

"What I like about customers is that they are the people with good problems that are worth solving. A lot of this stuff is commoditized or becomes commoditized quickly. So much of what we do is specialized. The specialized stuff is more of a challenge and brings a lot more value-added. As we develop a good reputation, we get more valuable problems to solve. That's how you want to grow, not just by doing more but by solving problems that are more and more valuable—because those are far more profitable."

One of those customers is Eric Hermsen at Tyco Telecom. "They don't do blue sky stuff. They are customer-focused—everyone from Lori right down to the people on the floor. All the way through they're just a pleasure to deal with. They're looking to do what the customer wants, not what they think the customer is looking for. I've dealt with other suppliers who come in and show me a new invention. We'll evaluate it, and it's just not something we're looking for. You'd think it was a well-defined space, but these companies still try to reinvent technology that will set them apart when, if they focused on customer relationships, they'd sell me better.

"They just execute really, really well. They listen. And they're really focused on delivering. That isn't true of every company. A lot of them just think the customer is a nuisance they wish they didn't have to bother with!"

What strikes me about all these businesses is not just that they avoid an adversarial approach to their customers—the kind of approach Lauri Union had to turn around at Union Corrugating—but they enter into a partnership with their customers, a partnership in which there is shared risk and shared reward. They aren't in a battle to win; they work together so that both thrive.

"I think it really makes a difference that all of us have been the client at some point in our careers," said Paige Arnoff-Fenn about Mavens & Moguls. "We know what it's like, and I think our interests are aligned. In year two, a CEO we'd worked with for about six months experienced a big change in her market, and she asked us if we'd put everything on hold for forty-five to ninety days. I said to her: "Given the new reality of your marketplace, why don't you just put the whole contract on hold? We can start the clock again when the business comes back." She told me that she'd hired agencies for twenty, thirty years, and they had always said that if you contract for a year, you pay for a year. I told her that if writing me a check wouldn't make *her* successful, how could it make *me* successful?

"We had one client, a software company, that came to the conclusion they really needed to bring the work we were doing for them in-house. They went away to think about who they needed to hire and came to the conclusion that they really wanted to hire our Mavens & Moguls consultant. But they said they felt guilty about pinching one of my people! I just said, "Look, don't feel guilty. If that's who you need, that's who you need." We weren't trying to make this company dependent on us; we were trying to make them successful! Those people are our biggest fans. We have so much work from people like that. If you do the right thing for the right reason, it comes back ten times."

Over the last three-year period Cecilia McCloy's ISSI has grown 400 percent. She attributes a significant part of this growth to the fact that 75 percent or more of ISSI's business comes from repeat customers. Sometimes this attitude toward customers evolves naturally, a function of the kinds of people that are employed and the attitude of the founder. But that doesn't mean it can't be taught or improved.

"Most of our project managers take a year-long course on the soft skills. And we have internal meetings where we focus on customer care to ensure that people are listening to customers the right way. We have a little course called The Customer Is Our Friend. We don't serve ourselves. We serve our customer. People often forget that. Women have a particular way of doing business and thinking about business, which is more nurturing than men. In the area of customer care and consideration, this can be very powerful. Success is everybody winning."

At the highest level, listening involves hearing what the customer wants and then understanding what the customer needs. It's a combination of technical skill and experience with empathy, that ability to see something through someone else's eyes. This has to go much deeper than politeness.

"When Diana Pohly started doing Continental Airline's in-flight magazine, she didn't just try to create a cool magazine, she made it Continental's voice," recalled Bonnie Rietz, who at the time was senior vice president for sales, marketing, and customer care at Continental Airline. "At Continental we believed that relationships were everything to profitability. Diana saw that you could make the magazine a forum where our customers could talk about their success. She put our best customers in the magazine and on the cover. Diana made that all happen. She understood what we wanted to achieve. She made sure she knew us and our customers better than anyone."

Knowing her customers so well gave Diana the insight and

understanding she needed to protect both her own business and her customer's.

"After 9/11 she came in to say that there were too many pages in the magazine and not enough ad sales to support them. She had recommendations as to how to change it. Month after month she'd been doing this magazine. She already had the full year planned out, but she still came in to tell us it should all be redone. Then she made it easy with options and alternatives.

"We always thought that if something was working, don't change it. Diana gently helped to persuade Continental that change was needed to stay effective. She took it to a higher place masterfully for a company that knew how it liked to do what it liked to do. She was looking ahead and thinking about how we could continue to do well, and she knew, before it was needed, that we had to change."

Call it nurturing. Call it customer service. Call it strategic thinking. Whatever you call it, this devotion to exceeding customer requirements lies both at the heart of what drives women and what makes them successful. So it is surprising and disappointing to discover that one of the chief obstacles standing in the way of women's businesses is getting the customers in the first place. In 1994, the Federal Acquisition Streamlining Act established a goal for federal procurement from women-owned businesses. That goal was a shockingly modest 5 percent. But today, more than ten years later, it hasn't been met. Currently, federal spending with women-owned businesses stands at just around 3 percent. Yet isn't it businesses like these that deserve tax dollars?

Nor is it only in the gigantic federal market that access to markets remains such an issue. Ask any female entrepreneur what she most needs, and her answer is simple: customers. Not just the government but Wal-Mart and Stop 'n' Shop; Lowe's, Home Depot, AT&T, Cisco, Microsoft, and Fortune 100, 500, and 1000 companies. And how much money do these large companies spend with women-owned businesses? The same sad number: Around 3 percent of what Fortune 1000 companies spend on suppliers goes to women's companies.[2]

I've never met a woman business owner who wanted or expected favors. They all know you earn your customers. They work hard and effectively to do so. And then, like Cecilia McCloy, they keep them. It is hard to imagine why any business wouldn't want to work with companies like these—unless they can't see them.

8. Improvisation

When I finally get through to her on the phone, much to my amazement, June Coldren is laughing. "Oh my God, it's ridiculous. It's been insanity. It's pretty wild. We evacuated New Orleans and moved west to Lafayette, and now it looks as if the storm is heading back up to us! They're basically evacuating everyone from Galveston right along the coast to Louisiana. All my staff who were evacuated here left yesterday to help evacuate *their* families. Another tidal surge, and everything will get wet all over again. I'm ready to move to Canada!"

June's family and her companies, Cenergy and Cenergy Logistics, were based in New Orleans when Hurricane Katrina hit on August 29, 2005. Everyone scattered to friends and family. But when it was all over, June still had two companies to run, companies that catered to the oil and gas companies in the Gulf of Mexico, themselves in turmoil. Three weeks after the storm hit, the Web site proudly announced that Cenergy was up and running.

"I love just winging it. That's just how I am. The logistics group—some of them live in Lafayette, so they came here and set up. Then we all got in touch and realized Lafayette was going to be the best place to be. We identified an office, set up, signed a lease, and moved in. Everyone who could get here did. The hard thing was to find places to live. There were no hotel rooms or houses to rent. One of the guys I work with had an extra house, so I feel like a queen because I have a house to live in!"

Not every business gets hit by a hurricane, but every business will suffer shocks and setbacks and successes it could not have foreseen. You can plan, do your research, and plan again. But the one thing you have to be able to do is improvise. As psychologist Simon Baron-Cohen wrote, "Women have no expectation of lawfulness."[1] Women don't approach business expecting it to obey rules. We don't think of it as a machine that, if we understood the physics well enough, we could control. So many descriptions of business and management carry the assumption that if you studied companies deeply enough and crunched the numbers long enough, you could glean the scientific laws of business that govern its behavior. But business isn't a science. You can't design or conduct replicable experiments. No two companies are the same. No two days are the same. Because the variables are infinite, those who start from the premise that there *are* rules are doomed to frustration. Where women start—without that expectation of lawfulness— turns out to be far more realistic. That doesn't mean women don't believe in plans or decisions. It just means that we aren't especially thrown when events render them meaningless.

"I hate business plans," admitted June Coldren. "I force myself to do them, but I hate them. So we've now made the decision that the logistics company will stay here permanently. And I can see that a lot of the business just can't get back to New Orleans. Most of my clients will move to Houston permanently. I know I need an office in Houston. It'll be small to start. When

my lease is up in New Orleans, I'll cut down that space and maintain a presence there but grow in Houston, so the company will
be based there. I have to follow my clients, and they are all moving to Houston."

She may hate plans, but June seems very good at making
them—fast. In the three weeks after Katrina hit, June restructured
her entire business.

"I just tried to sit back and think about how to start again. I
made the big decision—which I probably should have made
without the hurricane—to have most of my corporate presence
in Houston. I've been traveling and continuing business as usual
because sales have to keep ramping up, and we have to appear
seamless."

With so much damage to rigs in the Gulf of Mexico, there is
plenty of business for Cenergy. It is a great opportunity if she can
rise to it and if she can stop the phones from cutting out and if she
can find a new school for her son and if she can get some sleep.

"Am I tired?" She laughs at the question. "Yes, I'm tired. It's
hard to sleep because my mind is racing."

Entrepreneurs and investors devote a great deal of effort to
trying to reduce the uncertainties endemic in business. They start
with a business plan, whose research, spreadsheets, and financial
models aim to eliminate ambiguity and to make success look pre-
determined. They may use personality tests in hiring, trying to
persuade themselves that each new hire is no risk. So much energy in business goes on trying to nail it down, make it static,
predictable, certain. But we all know that business is subject to per-
sistent, even sometimes violent, turbulence. Operating in such a
volatile environment, efforts to eliminate uncertainty may be fu-
tile. Instead of trying to plan for every eventuality, it can prove
far more effective to develop skills of improvisation.

When I was recruited to run my first high-tech company, it looked like a consumer business. When we discovered the software wasn't robust enough for that market, the company evolved into a corporate software business. Lacking the skills and contacts for that market, I hired a CEO who had them. My next company developed a consumer product that was too hard to differentiate from competitors. So we redesigned the product, restructured the company, and, in ninety days, we finally had a winner. I could have complained that none of this conformed to the plans I'd been shown when recruited, but to what effect? It seemed more productive to keep learning.

We live in an economic environment where everything changes all the time, where waiting for every last piece of data makes you too slow, and where new markets don't obey predictions. In this environment the goal is not to avoid mistakes but to learn from them fast. Flexibility is key. There is no point insisting that something like a hurricane, a recession, or 9/11 should not have happened. Devoting resources to trying to predict change wastes both time and money. Leadership requires dealing with things as you find them.

When Adrian Guglielmo started her company, Diversity Partners, she didn't have a business plan; she just had an idea and a passion. "One day I walked into a graphic arts school that had all deaf people in it. And I said, 'I'm home.' My grandparents were deaf mutes, and I realized I had been raised in a deaf culture. The deaf have their own culture because they have their own language. I started talking to people and found out that there was an 80 percent unemployment rate in the deaf community. I had to do something about it, so I started a marketing company and hired deaf people. I started the first for-profit corporation for people with disabilities in America."

Adrian is a warm, direct, and enthusiastic woman who spent much of her early adulthood uncertain about who she was and what she wanted to do. She never went to business school, and there was nothing in her background that told her she could succeed. She had passion, and she understood the culture she was dealing with. What she didn't have was a wardrobe or a babysitter, but she didn't let those things stand in her way. "In 1996 I got a meeting with American Express, and I knew nothing about walking into corporate America. And I went into my closet: No business clothes. And I had a babysitter coming and you know what that's like—of course, the babysitter never showed up. So I got myself together in a mismatching outfit with a two-year-old in tow. It was the most embarrassing moment of my life. Ten men, with a two-year-old, wearing not exactly a New York City business outfit.

"My two-year-old was going in and out of the table until this one man put the two-year-old in his lap and gave him a yellow pad; the kid scribbled through the rest of my presentation. If I met that man today, I'd buy him a steak dinner. I was able to get the first big sale of my company. It was for $20,000 worth of mouse pads. I didn't even know what a mouse pad was and kept wondering why Amex had such trouble with mice. But I just said yes, I'd figure it out. Nowadays we get sales of $2 million, but that one was so important."

Adrian will be the first person to tell you about all the mistakes she made along the way. "I would call my autobiography *What Not to Do in My Business*. I got a home owner's loan. I signed for personal things. I signed my husband's name to things. I borrowed from everyone. I didn't pay taxes one month and paid them later. I held off on important bills. I learned very slowly. I was tortured. I *learned* from my mistakes."

What's impressive about Adrian is that she didn't learn just not to make the same mistakes twice. She grew. She came to see that while she was employing the deaf to produce marketing products, she was also developing a unique understanding of their community. She saw that the deaf represented a meaningful market—some 28 million people in the United States alone. And she parlayed that into significant consulting contracts with companies such as Avis, which enabled her clients to serve a market they'd never seen before.

No business plan could foresee this or persuade others that it was possible. That isn't to say that plans aren't important. They are. Plans keep everyone on the same page, focused and disciplined. The sheer act of writing them sharpens how you think about your business and its priorities. But no successful entrepreneur has ever succeeded without being willing and able to change course.

On October 21, 1997, Rebecca Boenigk took her company, Neutral Posture, public. Her ergonomic chairs had made her the first woman to trade on NASDAQ. She retained majority ownership, but she went public because she wanted to raise money for expansion and acquisition. At the time, the strategy made perfect sense. The IPO raised some $6 million, and she successfully concluded one very profitable acquisition—but that was the last thing that went according to plan.

"We were a manufacturing company, a traditional bricks-and-mortar business just when dot-coms became so fashionable. We suddenly found that we were everything the market didn't want in a company! So, of course, our stock went down and down." Using the password NASDAQ had provided so that she could see who was making a market in her stock, Rebecca discovered that her underwriters were bidding low to buy and high to sell—in other words, they were providing no support to the stock at all.[2]

Day-to-day running of the business turned from a pleasure to a poison. "The head of the board of directors had said he would run the board and I would run the company," recalled Rebecca. "But then he started telling the other directors that he was really running the company and that I didn't know what I was doing. The board was full of cronies. Some of the guys didn't think a woman could be competent. They were all over fifty, and they just thought I was silly. I was only thirty-two years old, but I was the reason the company was big enough to go public in the first place!

"I'd go to these board meetings, and these guys who knew nothing about my industry would question my ability. One guy was in the furniture industry—but home furniture, not office furniture. The rest knew nothing, and they'd abuse me for four hours. You're used to making decisions for yourself, and fast, and then the board would say you have to wait for the next meeting, which wouldn't be for ninety days!

"They wouldn't let us have a 401(k) plan for employees because they said it wasn't in the interests of the shareholders, but how can it not be in the interests of the shareholders to have happy employees who stay? And they said they wanted us to change our dress code! We are in the middle of nowhere in Texas, and they wanted us to dress up!"

Nothing about being a public company suited Rebecca or Neutral Posture. As the stock fell, the acquisition strategy collapsed. Rebecca's thrill at being the first woman to lead her own IPO faded fast. She could have railed against the unfairness of changed circumstances. Instead, she recognized her mistake and set out to fix it.

"It was one of the easiest decisions I ever made, but it was harder to go private than it had been to go public. We had to keep going back to the board with each improved offer. Going private ended up costing us as much as going public had, but we had managed to retain control and had cash in the bank, so we could do it."

Was the decision to go public a mistake? It made sense at the time, but then the times changed. And Rebecca probably chose the wrong people to work with. She learned a lot from her mistake, but she doesn't dwell on it. She has used the experience to move on. "It's nice to be able to say that we were traded on NASDAQ," she said. "It speaks to our strength and our stability. And we were able to go private again because we always kept majority ownership. We had a big party when we went private. We had everyone in the cafeteria and opened some champagne. And we went back to our old dress code. Now? The future looks wonderful. We weathered a huge downturn in the furniture market, and we weathered it better than most. And we are growing again. We have set ourselves some pretty tough goals, but we can do it."

Rebecca certainly learned the primacy of values and the danger of working with people who don't share yours. She learned how to make a course correction fast. She learned that she was better than she thought she was and that she didn't need a board full of middle-aged men to run her business for her. She knew what she was doing, and her confidence grew out of those mistakes.

Not all companies experience the extreme highs and lows of Neutral Posture, but behind every smooth narrative of business success is a lot of stomach-churning uncertainty. Doris Christopher says that on her way to do her first demonstration of kitchen utensils for what became The Pampered Chef, she nearly pulled over to a phone box to cancel. She really had no idea how it would go or quite what she would do. Even ten years later, with substantial success and experience under her belt, she keeps being surprised. Four hundred percent growth is a terrific achievement, but it isn't easy to manage. In 1990, having launched a big recruiting drive for the kitchen consultants who demonstrated Pampered Chef utensils, she found the company overwhelmed. She understood that more consultants would mean the company needed more inventory, and there wasn't time to build up enough stock before Christmas. No inventory would mean seriously dissatisfied customers, which would damage the company's reputation. But no CEO on earth likes to say no to growth.

"Dear Consultants," wrote Doris. "The incredible growth we have experienced is evident to us at the home office on a national scale. . . . Growth, however, needs to be managed.

"We will put a temporary recruiting 'hold' into effect beginning October 1, 1990. Our expectation is that this will extend until January 1, 1991."[3]

What a tough decision to make. Who ever read a business plan that forecast a freeze? And yet, as she told it, it was clear that this was an achievement of which Doris Christopher was rightly proud. She didn't say that she should have planned better. She knew she grabbed the right solution for the moment, one that protected her brand and her reputation.

What is so impressive about the way these women handle such a wide variety of crises is that they manage not to be defensive. They don't try to hide or to justify mistakes. They recount such stories not in the spirit of breast-beating or even of humility, but because they are stories of recovery and growth. "Look how much I didn't know," they seem to say, and "look how much more I know now."

At Delaire, Lori Hallock's whole team has to improvise. It isn't just a leadership skill, it's a company skill.

"In the last few years we've learned how to work through things as a team. Some people find it hard working here because they come with a 'it's not my job' attitude. But here, if it needs to be done, it *is*. This is something we've learned.

"When the telecoms market went down, we decided to retrain people in military fiber. We didn't know there was a war coming; we just knew we had to find a new market. But it wasn't easy because we needed ISO [International Standards Organization] certification. At first we hired someone from a big telecom company to help us with it, but it became obvious she couldn't get the job done. We were determined to do it, so Roni had to stop doing her HR job and become our Quality person. She spent a whole year getting us up to the right standards. Other companies began at the same time as us and are still working on it today, and we've been certified for six months. Now we can go for systems integration work, and we couldn't have done that without the ISO certification."

When you ask Lori how she learned to run a company that outlasted some of the telecom giants surrounding her in New Jersey, she'll be frank and say that she made it up as she went along—and the rest of her team followed suit. You won't hear one of them saying that something isn't their job; if the company needs it, they do it. This doesn't mean they're amateurs. They wouldn't be supplying the likes of Cisco, Alcatel, and the U.S. military if they were. It does mean that they can adapt fast. They are helped by being strikingly free of preconceptions about how things ought to get done. They don't expect the world to follow rules.

"Improvisation is having common sense, the most important ingredient in business," insisted Thermagon's Carol Latham. "You can't lock me into a plan. It's okay if the plan is dynamic and flexible, then I'm okay. But I find plans threatening. They try to stop you from thinking. And in business you have to keep asking: What's the right way to go? You improvise all the time about how to go down that road.

"You put your life on the table. When I left BP, I left all the fancy tools behind. I had to make my own tester for thermal resistance. Some of the data wasn't as solid as it could have been, but I couldn't afford the equipment to get perfect numbers. I just studied some of my competitors and knew, even with my rough tools, that I was getting better results than they were. The test is *so* difficult. It is hard to say the test number is absolute. And I couldn't go to conferences to hear what other people were saying because we had no travel budget. But I got the big things right—even with my own equipment."

When Intel called her with their Pentium problem, she knew this could make her business. So when they asked if she had a business partner in the Far East, she answered "no problem—I'll get one before you leave for Asia." And she did.

"Well of course I had to get one," she said with a laugh. "And I worried a lot because I hadn't met him. I worried whether he'd be honest, whether I could trust him. But I needed someone right away. And he turned into a real friend."

Improvisation is hard because no one can tell you that you are doing the right thing. So few businesses are really alike, and what was true for last year may not be true this year. In an ideal world, should Carol Latham have said she'd get a Far East agent when she didn't know one? Of course not. But she didn't live in an ideal world. She lived in the real world, full of contingencies in which one thing may not lead to another and in which there are always plenty of people eager to tell you that you are wrong.

"One of the things I did get right," said Carol, "was I knew how to price it. I knew what I made was important; we had a unique position, and I knew how to price it accordingly. One of my competitors once said to me: Your stuff is too expensive. And then years later he told me I was a pricing genius! We were always profitable. Even when the tech market collapsed, there was never a year we didn't make money."

Geraldine Laybourne has three mantras when it comes to her big business decisions. First: Be a sponge. Listen well. In her case, it's to the audience. In any business you have to listen hard to your market and listen in person; don't just read transcripts or summaries. Talk to your market and take its pulse. Second: Explode the myths. Some people, such as Geraldine Laybourne and Carol Latham, do this naturally. They're intrinsic challengers of the status quo. For others it is harder and feels scarier. But questioning what everyone tells you can be a great way to identify an opportunity where others can't see it (as June Coldren did with Cenergy Logistics). And third: Expunge the naysayers. This doesn't mean that you should surround yourself with toadies. It does mean you have to get the pessimists out of your face. All improvisation is and has to be fundamentally optimistic.

These women stuck with what worked but were prepared to throw away the rest. They were both flexible *and* stubborn; that's how improvisation works. That's the contradiction that every business faces and that women seem to be able to straddle with ease. To succeed you need to be focused and disciplined. Otherwise you dissipate your effort, confuse your workforce, and fail. But if your thinking is too rigid, you fail to respond to changing conditions and also fail. Somehow you have to be both rigid and flexible, focused and responsive. What strikes me about all the women entrepreneurs I've met is that while they take responsibility for their decisions (good and bad), they aren't defensive about them. What they are thinking about all the time is not what they want to do personally but what is best for the business. However wild and unpredictable improvised decisions may appear, they make sense when they serve the company, not just an individual in the company. The big, often public decisions I've seen women make successfully are never about them but about what is best for the company. This means they can be very painful.

"We were trying to do convergence," recalled Geraldine Laybourne of the early days at Oxygen, "but the cultural convergence was impossible. The TV people and the Internet people just couldn't talk to each other. We had nothing that was working that we could build on. We had seven hundred new people working together, and at best we got some pockets of success. So we had to shut it down."

Geraldine's decision to abandon the Internet was very public and very painful. It also meant losing some tremendous talents that she admired and loved working with.

"We had some great teams with some phenomenal people. And it was hard unwinding all of that. I hate losing gifted people, but we had to do it. We couldn't have been successful any other way. I wake up every morning, and it's a new day. I can go to bed downhearted and dog tired, and when I wake up in the morning, it's a fresh start."

I am not sure you can teach this kind of resilience, but it's clear to me that women have it in spades. Where does it come from? From parents, from childhood, sometimes perhaps from desperation, and certainly from necessity. In my own life, I have probably learned most about improvising from my children. I may make plans for them, but they're irrelevant in the face of developing personalities I have never been able to predict. They may eat only pizza for months, and when I finally cave in and buy a gross, they switch to omelettes. One year they hate school, and the next year all they want to do is overachieve. Late nights are a disaster this week, but next week we sail through them without a murmur. This doesn't mean that every day is a blank page. We have a routine and core principles that everyone understands.

In families as in business, values are key. Values aren't improvised and they don't change even if the business and its products and markets do. Values help to improvise the right kind of decision. They provide the framework that makes decisions coherent. When Rebecca Boenigk took Neutral Posture public, it made sense as a means to strengthen the company and bring added opportunity to her employees. Taking the company private again did the same thing. Circumstances had changed. Values had not.

This matters just as much or more when women are very successful. It may be easier to see the need to improvise when disaster strikes, but it is just as important when success strikes. Women are often criticized for being unambitious. They are less likely to launch their businesses with grandiose schemes for world domination or instant wealth. That doesn't mean they're unambitious, only that they come by their ambition differently.

"Big came to me," said Doreen Marks at Otis Technology. "I didn't aim big or small. It just happened. I just kept saying, 'Why can't you do it this way?' I'd be sitting at the kitchen table, fiddling with a patch, and my dad would ask what I was doing. I'd say, 'Well, why can't you do it this way?' And a few years later the Patent Office said it was the biggest advance in gun cleaning they'd ever seen!"

The same story could apply to the company itself. Doreen has done just about every job at Otis, from manufacturing to assembling to accounts receivable. She has redesigned the company as relentlessly as she has redesigned the product, constantly searching for ways to make it work better. That process of improvisation, coupled with Doreen's absolute commitment to quality, explains the company's success. Otis's growth hasn't been planned, it's been improvised.

Eileen Fisher would say the same of her business, that it has been through "many incarnations." The company has undergone phenomenal growth—82 percent in five years—but to sustain that growth, the business has had to change and change again.

"Every time we made mistakes," said Eileen, "we learned and got back to who we were. That is how we learn. That is how life is. I read one time that the most successful people just made more mistakes. We think it was all easy, but really the great people just made more mistakes and learned more."

Eileen pulls no punches about how painful and confusing mistakes can be, both for her and for the company. But she's never thought the way to handle it was to design some rigid structure that would try to eliminate mistakes. Instead, her company's success owes a great deal to her willingness to keep on improvising.

"For me," she reflected, "it was really having to think about what I contribute and what others do. As the business was growing, I kept having to reposition myself vis-à-vis the business and the people. You are not static. This is a really important point: The business grows up around you, and it is *you,* not it, that has to rethink position. It's just like with your kids: They are changing, but it's you that has to keep responding to that change."

It is very tempting when the business world is in turmoil to cleave to rigid rules and structures. It is human nature to yearn for the stability they purport to offer. It is only in being highly responsive to that change and being willing to rethink and reconsider, to keep asking Doreen Marks's question "Why can't you do it this way?" that real growth and success occur.

The classic business narrative tells of planning, discipline, determination, and serendipity, all ending in success. It usually features a titanic individual who magically manages to make all the right moves. By the end he is rich, famous, and has a gorgeous young wife. The scientific business narrative boils down enormous vats of data to extract five or six formulae that are proven to succeed. The implication of that story is that if you can be rigorous enough, crunch enough numbers, and follow the rules to the letter, you, too, will become handsome, rich, and well married.

What my time with female entrepreneurs showed me was that these are both fables. Modern myths. Yes, planning, discipline, determination, and number crunching are important parts of business. Without them you probably won't succeed. But neither will you succeed if you can't make it up as you go along and if you resist evidence that challenges all your plans. Real growth comes from mistakes, learning, and improvisation.

In Louisiana, June Coldren lived the weird mixture of planning and improvisation minute by minute. It wasn't easy, but I sensed that it was strangely exhilarating.

"There is no way not to be focused right now. What am I supposed to do? Walk away? That would be stupid. We've lost a lot, sure, but there's everything to win. Everything. And we can do this."

In business, as with hurricanes, no one ever quite knows what will happen next.

9. Help!

Carmen Castillo comes from a big family. "I have so many brothers and sisters," she said, "that really I've been on my own since I was five years old. We were a poor family, as poor as they come. And so I came to the United States in 1992 because I wanted to learn English and because I thought this was still the land of opportunity. I'd never have a chance in any other country, so I came to America all by myself."

Carmen was known as the "blond sheep" of the family. Being Spanish, her blond hair was unusual, and so was she. While her siblings stayed in Spain, she always knew she'd do something completely different. Arriving in the United States, she was not entirely without resources. She spoke a couple of languages (although not yet English, which today she speaks with a strong Spanish accent), she was a qualified chef, and she had a few friends. One of them was in Buffalo, New York, dying of cancer.

"She was one of my best girlfriends, so I went to visit and to help with her three kids for a couple of months. In the meantime, to make ends meet, I got a job working as a chef, and one day Richard Stenclik and his son came in for dinner. They liked the food so much that they asked for me. I came out, and we started talking. We had a nice conversation. We just had real chemistry."

When you meet Carmen, this isn't surprising. She's an ebullient conversationalist, full of warmth, intensity, and tremendous vigor. Carmen may not have had many resources in 1992, but she did have an idea—and better than that, she had nerve. So she asked Richard to help her get her idea off the ground. It was the single smartest thing she ever did.

Women aren't usually very good at asking. The fact that we don't like to ask for more money is one reason we remain underpaid and underpromoted. The fact that we don't like negotiating is one reason we tend to lose out in divorce settlements. Much of our socializing militates against asking: We are supposed to sit quietly and wait—to be asked to dance, to be asked to marry. Traditional definitions of femininity emphasize passivity and patience.

In business this could be fatal. But it all seems to change when women become entrepreneurs. Suddenly, we are emboldened to ask for help, information, insight, advice. It is a tremendously important and even lifesaving transformation. In fact, research shows that women are more likely than men to turn to outsiders for insight and advice.[1] I believe that we grow bolder because we don't feel that we are asking for ourselves but for "the idea" or "the company." We are acting on behalf of others, and in that spirit we're relentless. Asking for help is one way of gaining collective wisdom.

Stanley Milgram, the psychologist famous for his experiments exploring the psychology of obedience, did some less well known work in the 1970s on the phenomenon of asking.[2] He instructed his students to ride the New York subway and ask fellow passengers to give up their seats. Many of the students expected to be attacked; others were too sick with anxiety to do the experiment. But what they found was that 68 percent of riders gave up their seats. When researchers repeated the experiment just a few years ago, the rate had risen to 86 percent. Milgram had discovered something immensely important that we underestimate at our peril: Most people want to help. You just have to ask. You get more opportunities and intelligence that way.

When Carmen Castillo asked for Richard Stenclik's advice, she scarcely knew what she wanted. She had an idea—and in 1993 this was a pretty new idea—that technology could be used to centralize vendor relations. She figured that big companies dealt with hundreds and even thousands of suppliers, and if you could centralize all those contracts, you'd have efficiencies and also immense bargaining power. Carmen wasn't a technologist. She knew no one. And she had no money. But Richard Stenclik helped her. He was, and is, the chairman of the Superior Group of companies. Superior began as an engineering company but since then has developed into a conglomerate of businesses that provide people, goods, and services for supply chain management. So Carmen's idea was as good a fit for him as her personality had been. But she didn't want to become a Superior company. Superior didn't invest in her company, and she still owns 100 percent of it. What she needed was help getting started.

"They helped me understand the way American business ran, the way that bureaucracies work, that Americans think. The way to run a business."

Asking for Superior's help was a long shot. Carmen and Richard knew each other only through Carmen's cooking. What made her think that he would help?

"Well," she said laughing, "I didn't know anyone else! And they liked me and trusted me and saw that they could make money from me. That is what business is all about. Richard said, 'You are a super salesperson. You have a wonderful personality and a wonderful idea, and I think you can make it.' I respect him so much. He waked up my soul and said, 'You can do it! You have nothing to lose.' And he was right."

Richard Stenclik's support didn't obviate the hard work implicit in the task Carmen had set herself. He simply gave her advice and encouragement. She would need them in the hard months ahead.

"I started from my apartment with the Yellow Pages!" She laughs at the memory. "Knocking on doors and just knocking on doors. I'd try to make appointments, and sometimes I just couldn't get one, so I'd just go there and wait until someone would see me! I just asked for a small chance. Allow me to try, to try just one of your smallest groups. And when they let me, I would put together a beautiful proposal. I got help then from Superior because without them I didn't have *anything*! And I worked night and day. I would do whatever the customer wanted. If they wanted me to find someone who spoke twenty languages, I would get them. National and international suppliers. Oh my God, it was as competitive as they come!

"It took a while to get a customer. First was Metro Dade county, and then I was able to get into IBM. And, you know, once you're in, you're in."

And while Carmen was busy delivering on all those gorgeous proposals, Superior was behind her all the way, helping her stay focused on growing her business.

"They gave me the infrastructure that allowed me to concentrate on sales and running operations. That is the best thing I ever did. Today, I still outsource some of my functions—accounting, payroll, legal, HR. I outsource all of that and pay them a fee.

They make a lot of money out of me, and it works beautifully. It is still the perfect marriage. I talk to Richard all the time. I respect him so much. They are based in Buffalo and I'm in Florida, so it's perfect. There's just enough distance. We meet once in a while and talk about the business. We are three thousand miles apart, so it works just great."

Carmen says she spent years working like a crazy person, but it paid off. Today, hers is the thirty-fourth largest Hispanic business and the twentieth largest woman-owned business in America. She has eleven offices around the world, including Beijing, Shanghai, and the Ukraine. Her business—having never received any investment—is immensely profitable and continues to enjoy double-digit growth. Carmen built this success herself, but she didn't do it alone. No one does. Help comes in all shapes and sizes, but no woman really succeeds or thrives without it. Some entrepreneurs fret that by asking for help they'll jeopardize their idea, exposing it to smarter, better funded people who will steal it. But as Milgrim's experiment demonstrated, people want to help. Secrecy is a very high price to pay if it excludes you from the vast cohort of people who are willing to help.

When Pat Loret de Mola left Merrill Lynch in order to build Trade Settlement Inc., she thought she had plenty of time. But then rumors reached her that Reuters was starting a new business that intended, like her own, to automate high-volume, high-value syndicated loans. She had no time to lose; any idea that she might have cherished about building the business from scratch had to go out the window.

"I really had no idea about technology or how to build it, but when I heard what Reuters was up to, I had no time to hire a technology team—I was so worried that Reuters would beat me to market. So instead I talked to friends about the problems I was having, and one of them recommended outsourcing to a Canadian company. Well, at the time, the exchange rate was very attractive so we just got going."

In her rush to market she believed she couldn't afford the time it would take to do everything herself. It was a decision that turned out to have tremendous advantages. Not only did she not lose time to market, but in *not* hiring a roomful of engineers, Pat ensured that Trade Settlement never became a technology company. It started and has remained a financial services firm. The product is driven by customers, not techno-lust.

Having worked in syndicated loans much of her professional life, there is little about the area that Pat doesn't know. She knows the business, and, just as important, she knows the networks that run the business. She could not have gotten a hearing from companies like J. P. Morgan and Citibank without having lots of contacts and being prepared to use them. Although not a naturally outgoing person, Pat has used her networks to great effect.

"The network has been essential. I wouldn't have gotten through the door otherwise. Some of the companies I work with had to wait until I passed my five-year mark. They needed me to show staying power. But I could get meetings with most firms. That's what helped me most."

Although women think of themselves as great natural networkers, there is some evidence that we don't use networks as effectively as men.[3] We tend to think in categories that are too strict, that only work colleagues can help us with work problems and only family can help with family. The most successful entrepreneurs I've seen don't make this mistake. They take help from wherever they can find it.

"When I first got started," recalled Jean Soulios, "a friend of my boyfriend's heard about it. He used to be an executive at Elizabeth Arden, and he looked at me and he said, 'Do you know what you are in for? You don't!' But he helped me anyway."

Jean runs Jean's Creams, a company that has invented, manufactured, and now sells a cream for breast cancer patients undergoing radiotherapy. "I went for a consultation before my treatment, and I was told that it would burn. So I asked what I could use on my skin. I was told there was nothing. Sure, there are creams at CVS, but they're mostly water, so they don't help at all.

"I'd always been good at making things. I'd always been interested in science and health food and all that kind of thing. I figured out what a cream would need. Then a relative of mine went hunting on the Internet to see if she could find someone who would manufacture the cream for me. (My husband had been diagnosed with cancer at the same time, and I was too busy caring for him.) Anyway, she found a doctor who'd left the profession and was making creams through a third party. I got in touch with him, and he advised me. Then we found someone who could do the manufacturing for us."

The product went through eight iterations until it was right. "My surgeon really encouraged me. She said my cream was marvelous. She told me that some patients have to interrupt their radiotherapy because the burning is so bad. But with this cream you don't, so that makes the prognosis better."

All along the way, Jean has found people to help her with Jean's Creams—friends, relations, doctors, people with advice, people who provided PR pro bono. Of course it helped that the product was something they believed in. But June has discovered what Milgram knew: People want to help. Sometimes the help an entrepreneur needs is moral support. It is not to be underestimated. Building a business requires formidable endurance, and nobody keeps going alone.

"I have several girlfriends," said Nadine Lange at Open Scan. "One in D.C. has been my best friend for over twenty years. She's a great moral supporter. And I have sorority sisters in Houston who have supported me all these years. You need that. You need it just to keep going sometimes. And my attorney, Susan, has been just wonderful. She has worked with lots of big businesses and has really protected me, sometimes from myself. She is very bright and has lots of common sense and a great sense of humor. She's succinct, to the point, and there have been times when she hasn't given me choices. You need that, too, sometimes. She started as my attorney, but now I count her as my friend."

For many women the biggest source of encouragement, help, and advice they get comes from their husbands, especially when those spouses aren't involved in the business and can view it with some degree of objectivity.

"My husband is my best advisor," said Lori Hallock at Delaire. "He's spent his whole life in corporate America. He's had a career that is completely different from mine. He works in a place where there are rules and processes and structures. It's not that we want to be like that, but it's really helpful hearing how he comes at problems. He has coached me, and he's been a good coach. The fact that he's in the energy business and I'm in telecommunications has helped, too. It gives him some distance to see things."

Lori also gets a third opinion.

"Herb is like a second father to me. He came to the company because we advertised for a QA [quality assurance] job. He came in to do the job, and it rapidly became apparent that he could do way more than he was letting on. But he was retired, and he just wanted something to do. But he's so smart, and he has taught me a lot. He's taught me to see that it's a business. He gave me the courage to deal with people better. He doesn't work here anymore, but he knows the company well. I still call him, and he still visits. He's just a very wise person."

A third opinion (the phrase was coined by author and advisor Saj-Nicole Joni) comes from someone outside a business who has expertise and experience but no agenda.[4] No matter how high the integrity of the individuals involved, advice that comes from those inside the business is always biased. Everyone has a point of view and some personal interest, no matter how team-oriented the company is. A third opinion, by dint of being outside the company, has none. Instead, said Saj-Nicole, it helps to drive exponential thinking and to bring in a flow of other people and other ideas. Asking for this kind of advice is a sign not of weakness but of strength.

At National Van Lines, Maureen Beal brought in Bob Seeler as her third opinion. Bob had worked as a senior executive for many of Maureen's competitors. When he retired, Maureen turned to him for advice and insight.

"What's so nice about Bob is that he just wants to help the company. He has no other agenda. Bob has worked with Allied and some of the other van lines. He knows the industry inside and out. We have total trust. You have to be careful what you say to coworkers, but I can say anything to Bob.

"Bob taught me not to let people dump on me. Upward delegation. People would come in here and just dump on me and then walk away, and I'd be left holding the problem! Now if someone tries to do that, I discuss all the possible solutions, and they have to work it out. I've made a conscious effort to let them vent and then help them see that they can find the solution."

At the Eliassen Group, Mona has always been on the lookout for help, whether from books or coaches. The most important of these has turned out to be Ken Dreyer, whom Mona first met as a coach but whom she subsequently brought in to facilitate monthly and quarterly meetings.

"I like other people's views, and he is great with the team and has helped me deal with a lot of people issues. Besides being a math genius—his father was champion of the South African chess team—he has run several businesses. He knows what the life of a real business is like; otherwise, I wouldn't listen to him!"

Mona said that Ken has brought a lot more process to the company, something she thinks it needed but which she herself wasn't terribly good at. This meant that Mona didn't have to become someone she isn't; she could remain herself while the company developed some of the skills she lacked.

"The great thing about Ken is that people really trust him. They will confide in him, and he will never abuse that. He gets a sense of what the issue is and can raise it without its being attached to an individual people—so we can fix things without anyone feeling they're on the spot."

At Trade Settlement, Pat Loret de Mola uses her advisor somewhat differently. Richard Goldberg has been a corporate lawyer in a leading New York law firm for forty-five years. There is almost nothing he hasn't seen. "I bring gray hair to the situation," he said. What he meant was that he has a lot of experience in the way companies are built and deals are done. But more than that, as an outsider with a considerable track record, he can say things that Pat just can't. "In the course of my career I've had to say very aggressive things on behalf of people I've been representing. Someone needs to tell them to move things along. I can press those things to a point where it's better than if Pat did it or had to carry it alone."

Richard isn't quite a third opinion because he does have an interest in the company; he is a private investor. He can afford to be outspoken because everyone expects him to protect his investment and because of the weight of experience he brings to the table. As such, he can often ask harder questions or draw more provocative parallels than Pat might do alone. But it isn't just in meetings that Richard is so important to Pat. He talks to her on the phone or over coffee a couple of times a week. She will blind-copy him on documents and e-mails so that he's kept up to speed. "Probably we see each other face-to-face on average once a week because we'll be at meetings together. If we haven't seen each other for a few weeks, we try to catch lunch. It's very informal."

It speaks volumes for Pat that she found and reached out to someone of Goldberg's experience. He knows little of her market, he said, but he knows a very great deal about how companies develop and how they need to be run. He is advisor, mentor, and coach. "Entrepreneurs sometimes don't realize how far the entity has come. I sometimes remind her that she is the CEO of this company, and it is becoming an important company. It isn't a candy store. Some people looking at her want her to be an inspirational person. I mentioned to her a while ago that she shouldn't drop her voice in certain moments, the difficult moments. You can't drop your voice. You're the leader."

He says of Pat that she is excellent at improvising, at figuring out what needs to be done next. And he has terrific confidence in the business. But what he brings to Pat and to Trade Settlement is a mental model of the stature the company is developing and of how Pat herself must adapt to that. "There are areas in which she's gaining experience, such as how to speak to finance people and to investors. No one starts out knowing how to do that. It's always an incremental buildup. But she just soaks it up like a terrific sponge. She's not passive; she's an excellent quick study and a delight to work with."

The logical extension of this kind of relationship is to have an advisory board. Many privately held companies abjure these; for them, part of the privilege of being private is not having to deal with boards and board meetings. But I've never seen a company that wasn't strengthened by one. When a board is made up of real expertise and genuine support, it is the third opinion multiplied: a regular gathering of external expertise harnessed to find what's best for the business. There is, it seems, almost no stage at which external advice isn't a huge bonus.

"I think I have to start running Trade Settlement as though it were a publicly traded company," said Pat Loret de Mola, "even though it isn't. It's a good discipline, and I think it keeps us focused on the right things."

On Pat's board sit the venture capitalist who invested in her business, the chief economist from the Syndicated Loans Association, and two outside directors. They bring industry expertise, much business experience, and also more outside perspective. Pat is making very sure that she doesn't get blindsided and that her business is never held back by what she doesn't know. She has done everything she can think of to plough collective wisdom into the company, to ensure that it knows more than she can alone.

"I started my advisory board when I was just starting the agency," said Beth Bronfman. Her advertising agency, Leibler-Bronfman Lubalin, is her first business; before that she had worked for large corporations such as Macy's. "Not only had I never run a business before, I didn't even know anyone who'd set up a business. I hadn't a clue! I used my father's accountant, and I asked my brother for advice about lawyers. Before I knew it, I had my own advisory group, and they really helped me in those early days.

"Then, once I was under way, I found that trade organizations were crucial because they had the means and the opportunity to collect all the research and all the data that big agencies did. So when I joined them, I had access to a lot more information than I could afford alone. I became very friendly with them, and it created a bond. Nowadays, I guess the groups I rely on most are the Committee of 200 (C200) and the Women Presidents' Organization (WPO).[5] They're both full of business owners, but they're all in different fields so they really bring a different point of view. And, you know, it doesn't really matter what business they're in; they all have the same issues.

"The thing about running a business is, you have to be a cheerleader every day. You have to create a wonderful atmosphere. And you need to get some of that energy from other people. You can't do it all by yourself."

Unsurprisingly, there seems to be a correlation between joining formal business organizations and growing revenues. Those women's businesses with revenues of over a million dollars are far more likely to belong to formal organizations.[6] Growth and help go together. There is an ever-growing number of organizations aimed specifically at female entrepreneurs; chief among them are the National Association of Women Business Owners (NAWBO) and the WPO. They go to great lengths to foster community among women, to share insight and advice, and to build networks that offer some counterbalance to the still heavy hand of old boys' networks. That doesn't mean, of course, that women don't also use more established business organizations to develop themselves. Both Karen Caplan and Mona Eliassen joined TEC for that very reason. TEC is an international organization of chief executives who work together to help one another's businesses. It claims that its member companies grow two and a half times faster after joining. It is impossible to know how far that growth rate is caused by TEC training—and how much it is that the self-starters who come to TEC are destined for growth anyway. The very act of joining a support network indicates that participants aren't afraid to ask for and take advice.

What is clear is that all these groups—NAWBO, WPO, C200, TEC, the eWomen Network, and many more like them—provide the kind of insight, support, and experience that no entrepreneur can do without. They also provide forums where it's easy to ask for help, but it goes further than that. Robyn Benincasa, a firefighter, Ironman competitor, and builder of world-class teams tells a story of a grueling desert race when one of her teammates reached breaking point and asked her to help. She felt honored, and she learned an important lesson: "Asking for help is a gift to the helper." It is often hard to tell who is helped more, the woman who receives help or the woman who gives it.

When you consider just how hard it is to start and run a business, you might wonder why people don't ask for help more often. Some people don't want to be beholden; some may feel that asking for help betrays one's weakness. Others fret over confidentiality. What all of these women have learned is that the benefits derived from asking for help far outweigh the risks and that asking for help is a sign of strength. Only fools think they know everything.

10. Staying Power

I n *A Whole New Mind,* Daniel H. Pink writes that "the keys to the kingdom are changing hands. The future belongs to a very different kind of person with a very different kind of mind— creators and empathizers, pattern recognizers and meaning makers."[1] These kinds of people cannot possibly measure their work or personal worth in hours. Their work must be about quality rather than quantity, from a richness of knowledge and experience, not the accumulation of face time.

If Pink is right, then his "very different kind of person" is not really so new after all. She has been around for quite a while now. She has a wealth of experience to bring to the business; it just doesn't all come from business. Much of it comes from life. It is from her life experiences that so many women learn one of the essential traits of the successful entrepreneur: endurance.

In November 2005, Edison Automation made it into the Inc. 500. For Karla Diehl this was a huge accolade, and everyone celebrated. But Edison's was no overnight success. The company is fifteen years old; it is hardly an overnight success.

"People hear about it, and they think it's so glamorous and

exciting. The Inc. 500!" says Karla. "But there is a price to pay. Mostly, it's the gutted-out feeling that gets you.

"At the beginning—well, if I think of all the money we wasted! If I had that now, I could retire." Karla laughs. "There were times when, if someone had said we could just get out without debt, I would have. But there are times when you just can't quit because then you'd have to declare bankruptcy, and as long as you can keep going, you have to. It's really all about staying power. You just have to keep going."

The mythology of fast-growth companies is that you start with a brilliant idea, execute according to plan, and turn up on the Inc. 500. The reality is utterly different. Building a company is not a sprint, it's a marathon requiring formidable stamina and determination. If Woody Allen is right and 80 percent of success in life is just showing up, then for entrepreneurs 95 percent of success in business is just staying in business. But where does that staying power come from?

A sense of humor certainly helps. What is so striking about Karla Diehl, however painful some of her memories may be, is that she laughs so much.

"Staying power is the only way we've made it. With each mistake you know more, so you keep going because now you know more. You always want to learn what your last mistake just taught you—and then use it to do better next time."

Edison Automation started out in Nashville, Tennessee, as a distributor of automation equipment, selling to construction and design companies. At first they handled fifth-tier manufacturers; then they moved up to third- and finally top-tier equipment. As Karla and her husband advanced the company, they were still improvising, figuring out what kind of business they were in, where they added value, and how they could distinguish themselves. Edison Automation didn't come into the world fully fledged; its owners had to discover what it would be when or if it grew up.

"We grew over time," recalled Karla. "It took us eight to ten years to get momentum, build a reputation, and learn how to deliver without losing money. And then in 2001 we entered the utilities market. This is a huge market where projects can run up to $300 million, say, for a water treatment plant. They wanted the plants to run themselves, but they didn't have automation experts. And by then this is what we were. What has made us successful is understanding the value we add and how to execute. It's not revolutionary; it's not changing the world. Anyone can do it if you have the persistence. That's really what's made us succeed—having the nerve and the stamina to just keep going."

In 2002, Siemens asked Edison Automation to distribute their equipment in Alabama and Tennessee. They now have five offices and sixty employees, and are struggling to manage their explosive growth. Because companies, like people, have life stages; each new stage has confronted Karla with new challenges, hopes, and fears.

"You get over a hump, and then there are new challenges. Management team struggles. Processes that were less important when you were smaller. People who can't grow, who just can't make the transition to the bigger company you've become. It's like mountains beyond mountains. I kept thinking it would settle down!"

Edison Automation is the same age as Karla's eldest son. This isn't just a coincidence. Karla could no more walk out on one than she could walk out on the other.

"When we started, I had a one-year-old. Now I have two kids, fifteen and thirteen. Their whole lives have been the company. I just didn't know any better—starting the company with a one-year-old. But you do what you have to do even though you get so tired. The company ends up being a bit like your kids: You just can't quit. And on some level, of course, you don't want to quit."

Karla's capacity to keep going may be, in part, physiological; after all, women live longer than men. It may also be due to her passion to build Edison businesses not just for herself but for her employees and her family. She might be able to quit, but she can't face disappointing those who depend on her.

Sometimes, entrepreneurs tell me, it's just sheer exhaustion that gets you down. But women like Karla just keep going. They have both physical and, perhaps more important, psychological stamina. This is where working for your employees is tested. When you feel like quitting, the real question is whether you can let your people down. It is for others that so many women do what every business requires: keep hanging on.

Worse than the exhaustion are the near death experiences that test your mental resolve, making you wonder if this time you've made a mistake from which the company can never recover. Every company suffers these crises. It is only years later that success looks assured or even inevitable. And then the catastrophes tend to get forgotten or overlooked, forgotten in the same way that pain is forgotten.

Today, with stores gracing most major malls and department stores, nothing about Eileen Fisher's business looks fragile, but it hasn't always been that way.

"I remember that moment—I call it my French terry moment—when you put the key in the door and think, 'Maybe this isn't going to work out after all.'

"It was the moment when we were having trouble with the French terry fabric that was our mainstay. At the time, all our clothes were made with it. And then we got a shipment that was inconsistent. It was better yarn, but it performed differently, so all the clothes came out too long. We shipped them anyway, and then we got caught in the middle of it. People were complaining; they were canceling orders. And it was at the time there was a mini crash in the stock market, so it felt as if the whole world was crashing down around us. Clothes were coming back from the stores. We were shipping things that weren't right. It felt like everything was falling apart. But we had to keep going."

That was in 1988. She phoned buyers and told them to send back anything they weren't happy with. She pleaded with them not to cancel their orders for the next season. She didn't have a solution to the problem, but she did just keep going. She did not give up because, she said, "people believed in us and loved the clothes. I didn't want to let them down."

Eileen confessed to many "French terry moments." In 1998, one of the problems the company faced was that department stores didn't know where to position the clothes. Some went into casual wear; some went into designer departments. That meant they were spread across two different floors, which was confusing for everyone. The company tried to solve the problem by embracing it.

"We tried to separate the line, to have two lines, one for casual wear and a higher end line that we called the New York line. We created two whole new product lines with samples—with the result that we just confused people even more. And ourselves. We got too big and complicated, and there were too many products. The whole thing just got a little crazy. We weren't editing the line. We weren't focused. We were overwhelmed with complexity.

"But what our customers had loved was the way that everything went together. They liked the fact that the clothes were a system and all worked together. It was a very scary moment because we could have lost the business at that point." Recalling the experience, Eileen shuddered. "That was a really intense moment."

In many ways the strategy was everything the company stood against: It was too complicated, too ornate. It was trying to follow the department stores' lead rather than cleave to the intrinsic values of the company. Eileen didn't know what to do, but she didn't quit. She kept going, kept rethinking the problem, trying to understand it and what it was telling her.

"We learned so much. We ended up finding a lot of new products we wouldn't have otherwise. We changed our positioning and went higher end. We repositioned the company so that we could sell more expensive things because our customers really appreciated them, and they really appreciated the way things went together. You can wear our sequined top with the trousers you wore to work—that kind of thing. We made a mistake: We were stretched too thin and had too much money at risk. We got offtrack, but we sorted it out. We got back to who we were, and we were even better at it.

"I don't think I've ever panicked, but I feel I often have moments of feeling I've reached my limit. That was definitely one of them. Every time I've reached my limit, I need to think about what I contribute and what others can do. Part of me wants to run away, but I also want to be responsible. You have to think: What do you enjoy? What do you do that others can't?"

On the face of it, you wouldn't think that Edison Automation and Eileen Fisher Inc. have a lot in common. One serves business customers, and the other serves consumers. One deals in high-tech engineering hardware and software, and the other deals in clothing. One has price points in thousands and millions, while the other sells goods in mere double digits.

And yet, as both Karla Diehl and Eileen Fisher told the stories of their companies' growth, they both remembered with genuine angst how close they came to losing their businesses. They both remembered extreme stress and an overwhelming sense of responsibility. And they both used exactly the same analogy to explain how they dealt with it: parenting.

"It's like your kids," said Eileen Fisher, who has two teenagers. "They keep changing, needing different things from you. You want to be there but not interfere. You want to give them responsibility but not let them drive too early. You want them to learn to cook for themselves but not when they're five years old. They keep rephrasing their needs, and you have to keep rephrasing your response. They never stay the same, and you have to keep being there for them."

"You're a parent. You can't quit!" Karla said. "And no matter what happens, you have to stay calm. As a parent or a manager, you do not have the luxury of panicking. You have to instil confidence even in the face of crises."

Far from seeing parenting as competitors for the time their businesses require (as so many male managers do), these women have derived profound lessons and strengths from their experiences as parents. Being mothers has not undermined their leadership. It has informed and strengthened it. It has helped them to survive those near-death moments that every company endures.

In her book *The Mommy Brain,* Katherine Ellison brings together a body of recent scientific research that points to physiological evidence that mothering does give women the ability to endure discomfort longer.[2] She goes on to argue that the key skills of motherhood—juggling, sheer capacity for work, dependability, getting people to play well together, conflict management, discipline, mentoring, and delegation—are exactly the skills required of business leaders. And she points out that as more and more jobs are automated, the jobs left over tend to be face-to-face jobs that require emotional understanding and stamina.

The parallels between parenting and leadership strike me as being far more than some aesthetic coincidence. And what impresses me about women like Karla Diehl and Eileen Fisher is their ability to transfer wisdom from one part of their lives to another. The ability to stay lucid as her company dissolved into complexity—was that something Eileen Fisher learned at home or at work? Karla developed the strength to carry on well past the point of exhaustion when her boys were tiny, but it stood her in good stead for years to come. Improvising in their families gave them both new sources of flexibility at work. Far from proving a distraction, parenting for these women proved an essential source of business strength and insight.

If the first rule of business success is to keep going, the second rule may be to keep believing in your company despite crises and despite people telling you you're wrong.

"When I told my mother what I was doing," recalled Eileen Fisher, "she was appalled and said, 'But Eileen, you can't even sew!' My father was terrified because he knew I knew nothing about business. I had a boyfriend that I had to leave because he was a real naysayer. I would talk about my fantasies, and he'd just tell me I had no business sense. I think the naysayer thing can really wear on you, and you have to get away from it."

Carmen Castillo opened her offices for business the day Hurricane Andrew approached Florida. "We opened in the morning and evacuated in the afternoon," she recalled with laughter.

"What can you do? If you believed yesterday, you have to keep on believing. The hurricane doesn't change your business idea. You have to believe in yourself, not the weather!"

Carmen's SDI may run one of the largest woman-owned businesses in the United States, but it took her thirteen years to get there. Not thirteen years of cataclysmic glory but of steady, incremental organic growth that demanded total commitment. She would argue that a key part of her success was her ability to keep believing.

Fellow hurricane victim June Coldren would agree. After Hurricane Katrina, she kept going. She did one other thing that may seem counterintuitive but turned out to be very smart: She went on vacation.

"I'd booked to go to France in October, so I went. I needed it! I didn't know how much I was going to need it when I booked it, but I needed it!"

After seven years in business, June understands that she is running a marathon. Even where triumph comes quickly, maintaining momentum requires years of hard work, focus, and discipline. If the first rule for business success is that you have to keep going and the second rule requires that you keep the faith, the third requires that you pace yourself.

"I have tremendous stamina," conceded Pat Loret de Mola at Trade Settlement Inc. "I have to have because, in banking, people often won't trust you until you've been around for years, so staying power is how you win credibility. But also I'm just not a quitter. I used to run marathons, and you do learn to pace yourself. As long as there's progress, you get the fuel to keep going."

Pat runs a high-tech business in the financial services sector. It is a hot company in one of the hottest parts of one of the biggest businesses in the world, but Pat is calm. She is utterly unmoved by the high dramas of burnout, all-nighters, and red eyes. As her advisor Richard Goldberg said, "Banks can't afford to work with companies that aren't going to become mature businesses." So Pat works hard—very, very hard. But she also works smart. And she takes time off.

At first glance this may not seem so striking. Or that at Delaire, Lori Hallock shuts the company entirely for the Fourth of July week. Or that Paige Arnof-Fenn warns her clients that she takes a month off in the summer. Or that Beth Bronfman takes Fridays off in the summer. Or that Doreen Marks takes time out to accompany her teenage daughter to Paris. But at a time when Americans are not using up their paid leave to the tune of some $1.2 billion a year and when so many large corporations seem to think that vacation, like lunch, is for wimps, it is striking that these women business leaders make a concerted effort to ensure they get time off.[3]

There are many who make the mistake of interpreting this as frivolity, a lack of commitment. Women's businesses are regularly underrated and dismissed as "lifestyle" businesses. Because these women have more than one imperative in their lives, it is assumed they can't really be serious. For those who believe that commitment must be an exclusive act, these women simply can't cut it. They just aren't tough enough.

It is pretty clear to me that these women and millions more like them are plenty tough enough. They are among the toughest people I've ever met, and they are nowhere near finished yet. They've been through multiple near death experiences and survived them—more than survived, their companies have endured. And they have been able to do so not because they want to demonstrate the macho bravura of superheroes but because they know that commitment can never be measured in hours. They know that productivity is not a linear function of time.

This has been understood for over a hundred years, since Dr. Ernst Abbe studied working time at the Carl Zeiss optical works in Germany. He found that reducing hours by more than 10 percent actually increased output. Following his lead, Henry Ford appalled his peers by moving production from a six-day to a five-day week. Output increased and production costs decreased. But this is so counterintuitive that it keeps getting forgotten. Instead, across America, law, accounting, and consulting firms measure work in hours. If you want to reduce your hours, you're more likely to be branded a slacker than to be rewarded for discipline. Women negotiating for fewer hours are regularly marginalized for their lack of commitment. Economists such as Larry Summers argue that women can't succeed because they aren't prepared to put in an eighty-hour week. But on the basis of a century's research, why should they? It's unproductive.

What Larry Summers fails to understand is what businesswomen like June Coldren, Eileen Fisher, and Paige Arnof-Fenn know in their bones: that to be innovative over the long term requires stamina. Not burnout. Not macho displays of overwork. They understand, too, that good ideas rarely come in the middle of an all-night work session; they're more likely to come when you're driving home. To be able to improvise effectively, your brain has to stay fresh. Staying power isn't just about not quitting; it's about true mental stamina.

Many people make the mistake of looking at women's businesses and seeing merely lifestyle occupations. Trapped inside a masculine mindset, in which home is delegated to the wife so the male provider can focus exclusively on business, they view women's way of working as somehow lacking in seriousness and commitment. In doing so, they are utterly wrong.

When she gives tips to aspiring entrepreneurs, does The Pampered Chef's Doris Christopher tell them to drop everything and just work, work, work? Quite the opposite. She tells them to remember that "it's only a business." Why? Because thinking about it as only a business gave her perspective. It clarified her thinking. It gave her time to absorb lessons from outside her business. It kept panic at bay. It meant she made time for her family who remained her "number one priority" right past the point when she sold the company to Warren Buffett.

Eileen Fisher loves talking about her company, but she also loves telling you about playing the piano with her daughter. This isn't just polite small talk. She uses the story to illustrate a leadership lesson she learned from her daughter. Not from business schools or a business book or a conference or the newspaper or CNBC, but from her daughter.

I don't think it's a coincidence that Karla Diehl's company and her children are about the same age. I think her nurturing the children nurtured the business. There is a real benefit to stopping work and going home. And the fact that Karla and her husband could keep going for so long to build their successful company was not despite but because they had children to remind them what it was all for and to help them develop the skills they needed to succeed.

A growing body of evidence shows that managerial excellence is correlated with *external commitment,* that is, better managers are more involved in activities outside of work.[4] This shouldn't be surprising. Effective leadership requires a wide range of skills and a broad range of life experiences. This is even more important today when so many work processes have been automated.

What remains? The human, emotional stuff: resilience, empathy, creativity, and endurance. The research data and the stories of business leaders, such as June Coldren and her ilk, displace the old macho assumptions that you succeed only by excluding other interests, that the price of success must be the sacrifice of everything that makes you human, which for women means their femininity. These women have succeeded, at least in part, because they have stayed the course. What helped them do so? Time off and family.

When I ran companies for CMGi, I was sometimes envious of my peers, all men, all with wives at home. They could and did stay at work late. When they finally went home, I imagined dinner all ready, clean kids who'd already done their homework, and a wardrobe filled with crisply ironed shirts. This was certainly not my life. I had to be home at six. When my husband got home from his work, we'd figure out who did dinner and who did child care. We were bound to find something to wear the next day, but it was sometimes a bit of a scramble. By comparison, my male peers' lives seemed quite luxurious. But then I started to notice something odd. They all left—burned out or thrown out. I seemed to outlast them. Then I realized that arriving home at six wasn't a problem; it was a godsend. Having dinner and talking—sometimes about business, and sometimes about anything but—gave me perspective. Sure, looking after my kids took energy, but they gave me energy, too. The same was true of my friends whom I still made time for. Far from competing with my work, my life enhanced my work. A whole life was what gave me staying power.

When Daniel Pink argues that we need a new kind of mind to serve the demands of the new economy, I don't think that that mind is nurtured, fed, or developed in office buildings. It draws its ideas from everywhere—from home, from kids, and from communities. Where did Eileen Fisher learn so much about responding to change? From her children. Where did Karla Diehl learn staying power? From her sons. It is not in excluding life but in embracing it that we find strength.

11. Money Isn't Everything

W omen don't go into this thinking, 'How am I going to make money?' said Nancy Peretsman. "Guys come in here saying I'm going to make money, that it'll be worth $200 million. Here's a comparable company, and look how fast they made money. Because it is driven by financial returns, they could just as well be making widgets! But for women, money is one product of female success, but it's not the only product."

Nancy Peretsman is a partner in one of the most powerful media investment firms in the world. Prior to joining Allen & Co., she headed the worldwide media investment banking practice at Salomon Brothers. She has been named one of Fortune's Fifty Most Powerful Women in American Business, and her colleagues, singing her praises, all say she's "gender-blind." Nancy, they say, will always do what's best for the business. She has no axe to grind, which makes her insight into women's attitudes toward money and toward success all the more compelling.

All the women business owners I've met take money very seriously. Maureen Beal may come across as a "people person" and Eileen Fisher may think like an artist, but they're both on top of their numbers on a daily basis. Anyone who thinks that since they are female they're not really into math would be in for a severe shock. These women know numbers inside and out, and they are very good at seeing beyond them. Money is a big part of business, but it isn't everything.

When talk turns to business and money, minds usually turn to venture capital. And when that talk includes women, much is made of the VC community's shocking failure to see, support, or exploit the strength of women's businesses. Much should be made of it. Fewer than 10 percent of VC partners are female, and less than 9 percent of VC funding goes to women's businesses.[1] And those numbers have been going down since 2002.[2] While the venture capital community draws so much attention to itself as the driver of innovation, creativity, and entrepreneurship, the fact is that it has failed to engage with the biggest innovation in the business world today: the rise of women-owned businesses. They may have a sharp eye for new gadgets, but new talent continues to elude them.

Having worked with a number of venture capitalists, and counting some of them among my friends, I attribute their lack of engagement with women's businesses as more a lack of imagination than outright hostility. There is a dominant cliché in the business world: the start-up run by emotionally stilted, twenty-something boys who eat pizza, work through the night, and change the world. It is a cartoon given iconic status by Bill Gates, Marc Andreesen, and, more recently, Larry Page and Sergey Brin, the founders of Google. Their success stories are true stories, but they're not the only stories. Not all business success is male, pale, and under thirty. Not all business success requires venture capital, either. For all the noise it makes about itself, the VC world funds a mere 1 percent of new businesses. All business growth requires capital, but that capital comes in many more shapes and sizes than the male clichés of start-ups suggest.

You couldn't find a more refreshing antidote to the cliché of the adolescent geek entrepreneur than Geraldine Laybourne. After creating *Nickelodeon* and *Nick at Night,* Geraldine Laybourne left Viacom to work for Disney, and soon after left to create her own television network for women, Oxygen. For a highly experienced and esteemed program maker, this wasn't an inevitable step. More routine might have been for her to set up a production company, feeding new product to any number of networks. Such a strategy would certainly have conformed to the image many VCs have of women—that they are less ambitious, less growth oriented, and more risk averse. But Geraldine deliberately chose the tougher, bigger challenge.

"I did it because I could. And because I could, I felt I had an obligation to do so because women weren't doing start-ups on a scale of business like this one. So I felt that I had to. I had to do it for my sisters. And I feel that I have a lot to prove. I'm a second child, and I will go to my grave feeling that I have a lot to prove."

Geraldine has raised more venture capital investment for her business than any other woman in America: a total of $500 million. Her funding has come from both men and women. Nancy Peretsman worked with her to raise this money.

"Gerry, I think, has accomplished what no other woman has accomplished. But it wasn't aspirational, it wasn't just a dream. She already had a very successful career as an entrepreneur. She had built *Nickelodeon;* it was built inside another corporation; she didn't own it. In building Oxygen, Gerry was in partnership with Marcy Carsey, who had built up Carsey-Werner, and with Oprah Winfrey, who had built up her own enterprise. They both put their own capital in on a scale that most mere mortals could not do. This really teed them up. Sure, there was a lot of talent, but if you took someone with only a line job that had never started something, you couldn't raise $500 million for them. This was a team of proven entrepreneurs."

However proven, even Geraldine recalled finding the world of investment banking somewhat daunting. She recoiled from a proliferation of jargon that was both forbidding and excluding.

"I think every profession has its jargon," said Nancy Peretsman. "To me there are two kinds. Some is necessary shorthand, to do with structural preferences, the mechanics of doing transactions. You can put those in lay language. But there's terminology that's associated with it, and once it's explained, it's not rocket science. It's not string theory."

She starts to laugh. "Now some people may choose to hide behind the jargon because it makes them sound as if they're string theorists! But you know, the first time you do something you haven't done before, there's a new language to learn."

Refreshingly jargon free herself, Nancy Peretsman recalls that even with the names and capital and track records attached to Oxygen, raising money was not, as she says, "all peaches and cream." Nevertheless, Geraldine and her team kept meeting or exceeding their goals. They kept convincing more cable companies to carry the station; they built up their subscriber numbers. They focused on building an asset, something that would have value to investors. It took time.

It was always going to take time. Oxygen required investment because it is impossible to build a cable network, and to survive during the years it takes to build audiences, without it. If you want to be this big, you need big backing. Many women eschew this route, not because they don't want to be big but because they fear the lack of control that so often accompanies size. Geraldine has been able to be smarter; as well as holding an equity stake in the business (together with her founding partners), she also controls the right to designate a majority of the board of directors. Geraldine could keep this degree of control because she had a luminous reputation and track record that people wanted to invest in. She wasn't a twenty-two-year-old kid, and her experience bought her more power within her business. That power grew as she hit and exceeded her business targets.

"We could raise money after 9/11 because we had outperformed and we had a promising business," Geraldine recalled. "No one else had created a unique asset in that time. Other companies were either digital or involved merely in retransmission. We are a valuable asset because no one owns us."

"The last financing round was a tough time," recalled Nancy Peretsman. "It was 2002, and markets were tight. But by then there was no argument that Oxygen was anything but an asset. There were discussions about how valuable it was, and that was both a function of the marketplace and where the business was at that time."

Today, Oxygen is profitable, and it has sailed past the magic number of 50 million subscribers in record time. In the cable business that number is a tipping point, signifying critical mass. It is, as Geraldine said, "when multiples start to kick in," and it's the number that proves that Oxygen works as a business. Money bought Oxygen the time it needed to prove itself. Not everyone can raise this scale of financing, but most don't need it. Oxygen did need it; there is no way to build a television station without large amounts of capital over a significant period of time. That such a capital-intensive business has succeeded augurs well for women in the future.

"All brand-new entrepreneurs have trouble raising money, but proven entrepreneurs can raise a lot of money. There aren't that many of them, and there are not that many proven *female* entrepreneurs. But as there are more and more, there will be more with a track record—and then it will be a lot easier."

So far, Nancy is being proved right. Nearly three out of four women business owners who had previously owned other companies had a high rate of success when seeking expansion capital for their businesses—whether in the form of investment or commercial loans.[3] It isn't a tidal wave yet, but it looks like a trend.

The scale of funding she has raised makes Geraldine Laybourne exceptional, but her ambition does not. Many women want to build big businesses, and many continue to find the capital markets deaf to their ambition. This may be due, as Nancy Peretsman surmises, to less experience—the inevitable penalty of being new kids on the block. But others try to explain or even justify it by saying that women just don't want to build big companies, and they don't want to grow fast. This is incorrect. Companies seeking venture investment, whether run by men or women, look pretty much the same: same sectors, same size, and same revenue goals and growth goals.[4] And in high-tech specifically, women-owned firms are more likely to be fast growing than men-owned companies.

The problem doesn't lie with the women, their ambition, or their track record. I think it lies with stereotypes. Female entrepreneurs don't look like geeks. They don't behave like Mark Cuban. They don't dress like Sergey Brin. And so it takes a formidable amount of intellectual firepower, connections, expertise, and sheer bravura to break through the mental model of how a successful entrepreneur looks, sounds, and behaves. The Kauffman Foundation calls this pattern recognition: "Over the years, venture capitalists develop a pattern of what has been successful for them, and if they have never invested in women over five, ten or fifteen years, they won't. It is almost as if a woman has to jump a higher hurdle because they do not exactly fit their pattern of what a successful CEO is like."[5] So Nancy Peretsman may be right: As more and more women succeed, it could get easier—especially when, like the women of Oxygen, they don't hide their femininity.

"With me," said Geraldine, "I think there was an element of 'What right does a program maker have to be an entrepreneur? And how dare she?' But I also think that being a woman has been a fantastic advantage because my biology means that I have the right brain structure, the right personality, the right love of process and love of people that's needed to succeed in this business. Lots of my male peers have to wear suits and fit in. I always did better at being me than others did at being someone else!"

Carol Vallone would agree with her. She raised $125 million for her company, WebCT. She did so in several rounds. It clearly helped that Carol, too, had a track record as an entrepreneur, and she is an accomplished, experienced saleswoman. But she thinks it also helped being female.

"Raising money is not magic. It is like selling anything. It is understanding what values your investors have, and what success means to them at that point in time. I also found, through my whole funding cycle, that people really wanted to help. If someone said to me, 'no we aren't interested,' I would say, 'What kind of people do you think would be?' And that is how I built my venture network. But it also helped that I was a woman because they didn't see that many women. So they always remembered me!"

The dominance that the image of venture capital exerts over

the public imagination is profound. As a consequence, women are often downhearted at the venture capital community's inability to recognize their worth. But the importance of venture capital is also wildly exaggerated. For one thing, VC alone is no guarantee of success. Nearly half of the VC-funded companies fail, whether counted by number or by dollars invested.[6] At the current time, when women-owned businesses are twice as likely to stay in business as others and when businesses owned by women of color are four times as likely to stay in business, most VCs are blind to the opportunities that women present. Business models in today's economy need to be more flexible than ever. The same might be said for mental models of what success looks like.

"I spent a year looking for capital in our second and third years. What I saw was a bunch of old school idiots who totally missed the fact that they were looking at a project that was obviously the way things would be going in the future. Maybe they overlooked it because I was a woman. More probably, they overlooked it because my plan didn't fit into their unbending formulas," said Kimberly Bunting at Business Access in Texas.

"Amusingly, at the time we were looking, I frequently heard that VCs were not interested in businesses that relied on government contracts (to which I replied, 'Hey, at least they pay'). This year when my company was getting a Spirit of Entrepreneurship award from an organization made up of many VCs, they gave me a presentation saying they just loved government business!"

Venture capitalists are relevant only to a minute number of companies. Less than 1 percent of all start-ups run by men or women receive any venture funding at all, and the vast majority of fast-growth firms are not in high-tech.[7] The sound and fury made by the industry has thrown into shadow the fact that most high-growth companies are started with less than $50,000 in capital.[8] Just because you aren't in the VC world doesn't mean you aren't serious about money or ambitious for your business. There are lots of other ways to grow successfully.

"I was very creative," recalled Eileen Fisher. "I did it a little at a time on a shoestring. I went to the Boutique Show and got my first small orders—at first just $3,000 worth. I had a friend who made the patterns, and she said I could pay her later because she believed in me. The next time I went to the Boutique Show, I got $40,000 worth of orders. But I had some experience now. So I borrowed money from people I knew—at some highly usurious rate like 2 percent per month. And I broke down production into two phases so I'd deliver some, get cash on delivery, and then have thirty days to pay my sewing people. And by breaking it down like that, I needed less cash than I held at any given point. I'd never done anything like this before. I was just responding to thoughts that kept coming to me. I just kept thinking: I have to do this. The orders are in front of me. It doesn't make sense not to do it. And I had enough passion to do it."

That passion isn't untypical. Eileen Fisher calls it a mixture of "backbone with heart." Nancy Peretsman sees it as one of the distinguishing features of female entrepreneurs.

"The women that I've helped or funded had one common motivating factor, and that is an absolute passion for their product and their business. And they can usually do a very good job articulating what they are building. Interestingly enough, whether or not they will be financially successful will be derivative of the argument for their product—which is to say, the money is a by-product of the vision, not the only end product. With men it's a much more mixed bag. Sometimes I'll get a financial entrepreneur in here who's just spotted an opportunity to make some money. That's all it is. But I have not yet encountered a woman who was just pitching a clever financial idea. They have a real passion for what they're doing, for what they're making."

The emotion that women invest in their businesses—the same emotion that makes them feel out of place in traditional corporate environments—is a huge asset. In many companies, passion and ingenuity have to make up for the funding that the capital markets won't provide. Women still receive only a fraction of commercial loans and SBA loans. The vast majority of their firms are grown on earnings.[9] But bootstrapping is much more than the means of last resort for funding a company, as Kimberly Bunting discovered when she finally gave up looking for investment.

"The advantages of bootstrapping have been important to Business Access. Our prices are based on our real expenses at the predicted volumes of business. When our revenues are affected, our expenses have to follow—and vice versa. There is a clarity of cause and effect that permeates our company. Quality assurance isn't a buzzword, it's a financial reality."

In other words, bootstrapping has kept Business Access very close to its customers. You could say the same of Open Scan, where the technology has been largely customer driven; or The Pohly Company, where customer focus is key to the company's competitiveness; or Delaire, whose customers know they're heard; or Eileen Fisher, who constantly scans her sales numbers to understand better what it is that her customers love. What Kimberly calls "the clarity of cause and effect" keeps these businesses alert, attentive, and customer-centric. Everyone in these businesses knows the central fact of business: All money comes from customers. Everything else is an expense.

All these businesses are very thrifty. Lurita Doan founded her business, NTMI, when Unisys wouldn't take her business plan for their business seriously. She started with $25, no customers, and no venture capital. In 2003, the business had revenues in excess of $210 million. She got there by being very careful. She always saved and reused her "sign here" stickers. She wouldn't pay for more than one color of Post-it notes and two styles of pens. And she insisted that letters being faxed be printed on photocopied stationery, not expensive printed letterhead. She estimates that such thrift sent an extra $100,000 to the bottom line. Like every female CEO I've ever met, she is a fanatical recycler.

Being thrifty doesn't mean being stingy. At Delaire the bathrooms are full of soaps, shampoos, deodorants, and soft towels. At Eliassen the kitchen is full of fresh fruit. At Otis there are barbecue pits and park benches. At Open Scan an inner-city warehouse is stylish with screens for cubicles and purple linoleum on the floor. At The Pohly Company there is wine and beer and bagels. And, more important, the companies provide phenomenal benefits to their employees. So none of them is deprived—but they aren't spoiled, either. They just have no sense of entitlement. They know exactly where every dollar comes from.

"I have to be as smart as I can to present my financial needs," said Elizabeth Deschenes at The Pohly Company. "The money is there for my projects as long as I prove I will use it wisely. What I have to think about is how my project helps build the company—because if I don't help build the company, we don't have a company anymore. Sure, you may think about 'What's in it for me?' but if you aren't looking at the bigger goal, if you aren't helping the company, why should anyone help you?"

Diana Pohly bought the business from its former owners who acted as her bankers. She paid the loan off in five years—faster than she needed to but slower than she wanted. The financial rigor and thrift that allowed her to do this permeated the company, giving it that clarity of cause and effect that Kimberly Bunting described and that many companies can only dream of. Bootstrapping doesn't just impart clarity. It also enhances determination and refuels the passion.

"If it's your own money and your own signature that is on the line," said Doreen Marks at Otis Technology, "you will make it work. The elbow grease from my family and me—we have worked a hundred hours a week, all of us, at times. Even at Thanksgiving we talk about business. It is such a part of our life. People ask me how many children I have, and I always say three: my firstborn child is twenty years old, and she's a gun-cleaning system."

Doreen laughs as she says this, but you know she's in earnest. She made kits after she finished waitressing; she made kits through college. Everyone in the family is paid the same way, based on sales that month. If they don't sell, they don't get paid. Sales and pay—cause and effect.

"I always think we are only one decision away from losing the company," Joni Walton said. "So I will never take a risk I don't know I can recover from."

Like many women, Joni is fiscally very conservative. In investment clubs, women tend to buy stocks and flip them less frequently than men. At times of economic uncertainty, they're less reactive than men, tending to build a strategy and stick to it.[10] In Joni's case, that basic tendency is exacerbated by her having started with so little. Success still surprises her. But she's not entirely accurate when she says that this makes her risk averse. After all, she started the company with what became a $100,000 loan from her former boss, Mason Bergh. That in itself was a huge risk. Even if the capital that started the company wasn't Joni's own, it may as well have been. Her sense of indebtedness and personal exposure may have made her cautious, but it also high-lighted what mattered in her business: not revenues but profits.

"All I ever thought about was profit. Always. Every day. Because profit was how I was going to pay Mason back. And even now that he's gone and I've paid back everything, I'm the same way. Revenues are wonderful, but nothing beats profit."

She is not in danger of forgetting that lesson, but just in case she does, Mason's photograph hangs in the reception area of Danlee Medical to remind her.

Every story I encountered contained the same moral: Don't focus on revenue, never mind market share. Focus on profit. And, indeed, the data show that women's businesses are building profits faster than men's businesses.

"I always thought more about profit than revenue," said Lurita Doan. "In fact, for years this has been one of my complaints about the Small Business Administration. Most of the contests for government contracting are all about top-line growth, but what makes a business able to succeed is profitability. I mean, what is the point of making $50 million with 1 percent profitability? You'd do much better to make less with more profit.

"A lot of it has to do with Wall Street, which gets enamored of numbers on the top line instead of thinking about your ability to propagate your business year after year. I think that women as a group do have more of the caregiver mentality, and we see ourselves as having to provide for others. Well, you can't do that with little or no profit. That's why we get so much value from our businesses."

I love Lurita's phrase about propagating your business. This, after all, is what profit is for. Profits matter because they do three things. They fund innovation, they buy time, and they make a company sustainable.

I haven't encountered any women-owned businesses where profits went to support a lavish lifestyle for the owner. I'm sure there must be some, somewhere. But all the business owners I met were strikingly modest—well groomed but not especially fashionably dressed and living in nice but not remarkable houses. (As Nadine Lange commented, "How many rooms can you be in at one time?") Some drove nice cars, but others, like Lurita Doan, were proud not to.

"I am sitting in my Saturn, and I am happy to sit in my Saturn. It has a sun roof, quad sound, a CD player, and four-wheel drive, and it cost $22,000. And it is a great car."

Most women business owners, such as Doreen Marks, take a salary based on sales. All are intent on plowing money back into their businesses. At Eileen Fisher, a minimum of 10 percent of after-tax profits is shared among employees as a way of recognizing their contribution and commitment. At Thermagon, profits have gone to fuel technology innovation and infrastructure: a larger manufacturing area and better, safer equipment. At Otis, profit has financed the glistening new factory that will hold more employees and produce more new products, based on more new patents and using robots to eliminate tedious, dangerous work. At Danlee, profits allow Joni Walton to look for new medical problems to solve with new supplies. The Eliassen Group is expanding; it has new offices in North Carolina, Connecticut, and New York City. The Pohly Company recently announced three new business units that will triple revenues over the next three to five years. Carmen Castillo of SDI is opening up new offices in Eastern Europe. At National Van Lines, profit allows Maureen Beal to buy more trucks that are better suited to the different environments in which her drivers deliver. At Neutral Posture, profits make it possible for Rebecca Boenigk and her team to introduce regular improvements to their ergonomic designs. Profit fuels innovation.

And profits buy time. Think of Doris Christopher freezing recruitment at The Pampered Chef. She could afford to forgo the revenue they might have brought in because she had plenty of profits to live on, and she knew how important it was for her to consolidate the company's operations and reputation. She used the time to move handwritten orders over to computers, to bring new warehousing onstream, and to integrate fully the newer consultants.

At NTMI, having profits in the bank meant that Lurita Doan could afford to take risks.

"Like everyone in government contracting, there's a belief that bigger is better because you get more credibility with the federal government. So you go after contracts that aren't really in your area of core competence. Once, we were offered a $22 million contract, and that really worried me because it was all pure hardware and we didn't really do hardware.

"Well, whenever I'm in trouble, I always go out to my garden. I have a huge rosemary bush near my deck, and when I was thinking about this contract, I looked at the bush and thought: That's my company. It was big, bushy, and 4 feet wide on top, but the stem was only about 2 inches wide. And that's what happened to my company. We didn't have core strength, the foundation to support all these different areas we'd branched out into. I needed to prune back. So I cut the bush back, and a few days later it looked as if it was thriving and not toppling over. It was supporting itself and growing.

"The next day I tackled the company. I said no to the government. They were stunned. They flew someone out to talk to me. They thought something else must be going on, but the truth was we didn't have infrastructure for this kind of thing. We would botch it. So instead I gave them names of the two companies that would do a better job. It was one of the smartest things I did because then I put all our energy and effort into our existing lines of business, particularly surveillance, and that really made a name for us."

After turning down the government contract and refocusing the company's efforts on their core strengths, NTMI's profit margin went from 6 percent to 17 percent, and the company was cited by *Forbes,* the *Washington Post,* and Deloitte as a fast-growing company to watch.

"I think that people like the gross numbers because they sound so fancy," Lurita said, "but what really makes a business successful is the bottom line. It's what gives you your flexibility, your seed money for new ventures, and your investment in your people and infrastructure—not to mention that you sleep better at night."[11]

Joni Walton concedes that at Danlee Medical Supplies growth is probably slower than it could be. "We grow as much as the business and I can both take. We grow so that I can control it." She is strangely apologetic about double-digit profit growth. Some of that is undoubtedly due to Joni's fiscal conservatism, but it's also because she wants to consolidate what she has built and she's in it for the long haul.

"I can't be here twenty-four hours a day. I can't let it consume my entire life. There are so many things I want to do with the business—I have got to pace myself."

It takes time to grow a business—time to integrate new people and processes, and time to embed a culture. And if you want that company to last, time is the only antidote to burnout.

"We were in the Inc. 500 last year," said Cecilia McCloy at ISSI. "Over a three-year period we've had a growth rate of 400 percent. And last year we didn't exactly plateau; we had a growth rate of 35 percent. But we are actually now trying to control our growth because what happens to many small businesses is that they overextend themselves. You have to be very careful.

"We have people who come in and say to us, 'You guys don't look frazzled.' They expect to see futons everywhere and people working in the clothes they slept in. But we want people to go home! It's about sustainability. For us that is important. Growth is important—we want to grow—but my hope is that we grow *and* are sustainable."

What is striking about all these businesses is that they are all growing fast, but they are growing reputation, credibility, and reliability as intently as they are growing revenues and profit. They are using money in the form of personal loans, bank loans, SBA loans, and lines of credit prudently and effectively, but not one of these women sees money as a sign of success.

"I don't ever think of money as a report card," said Lurita Doan. "I wonder if that is a guy thing. I don't know any women who use money as a measure of success. I know many guys who do. If one guy gets $10 more in a sale, it really bugs them. I know so many people who have money that I don't see how anybody could think it measures success. There is no way my company was worth in 1997 what it's worth today, because surveillance is such a big thing right now. But that's just timing. Nonobtrusive inspection—seven years ago no one knew what that was! That's what has added value to my business. But that isn't what I did; the world did that."

When I asked Geraldine Laybourne what success looks like

to her, despite having made Oxygen profitable for two years running and despite having outperformed all her goals, money was no part of the answer.

"What does success look like? It looks like we have truly gotten under the skin of women aged twenty to forty and that they've understood what we stand for. Most people would say ratings, but I think it's deeper than that. For me it really is when they understand us. In part we measure success by how effective our creativity is, but in the end I think success is a gut feeling that you've met your audience."

Over the last five years, despite a rocky economy, Eileen Fisher has seen 82 percent growth—success by anyone's measure. But that isn't what she thinks about. She thinks about whether or not the company will be able to roll out a stock purchase plan for employees and whether or not people still love her clothes. Success, she says, is holistic.

"Success is when you see people wearing your clothes. It delights you, and you know you are serving the customer, and people want it and want more, and people are happy, and the company is happy."

For others, success is about maintaining a culture, being able to employ more people, being able to provide more benefits, being able to invent more products that make the world safer, cleaner, or more fun. To be successful requires money and astute management of money, but it is not an end in itself.

If the male concept of business is dominated by money, as Nancy Peretsman has observed, then it makes sense that men might be blind to entrepreneurs who see money as only part of the business rather than its whole. What that suggests is that men's thinking about business tends to be narrower and less ambitious than women's.

"Money cannot possibly indicate whether you are smart, whether your work is valuable," said Lurita Doan. "To me, if I want to know whether I'm successful, I ask myself: Is the world better because I was here today? The answer should always be yes. That is success.

"Business is one way that you make the world a better place. Take it as a microcosm. Because I run my business well, I am frugal, we can have a fantastic quality of life for our employees. That is a kind of philanthropy. As a company we can be philanthropic, too, and that is leading by example—and then you encourage employees to do it on their own. Put all of that together, it makes the world better because of what you've done with your business."

The glamour and self-promotion of the venture capital community have done much to promote the idea that real business is about money and nothing but money—making mountains of it fast. But that's just one model. It's not the only model and it's not the only successful model, and it's not relevant to the majority of businesses in the United States or, indeed, around the world. Women's businesses do well to remind us that business and capitalism have always been about much, much more. Business leaders such as Geraldine Laybourne, Lurita Doan, Eileen Fisher, and millions more like them are much more ambitious than the money they create can convey. It should come as no surprise that, aiming higher, they achieve much more.

Part 3

The Only Failure Is Not to Try

12. M & A: Marriage and Acclimatization

In 1998, Universal Learning Technologies was just over a year old. It had been founded by Carol Vallone to build software that would put university course material online. This was Carol's second business. A level-headed, down-to-earth entrepreneur, Carol is neat, organized, and highly driven. Looking more like a bank manager than a techie, she radiates certainty and calm, and she's thinking all the time. She's an optimist. When she launched ULT's first product, that optimism seemed justified—except that everywhere Carol went, she encountered her competitor, WebCT.

"The reaction we got to the product was 'This is great technology, but everybody is talking about WebCT,' recalled Carol. "Well, we had watched Murray Goldberg, who was a computer science faculty member at the University of British Columbia. Under a grant he had developed WebCT, and then he had gone around the world and talked about it and was pretty much giving it away. He had a group of engineers; he had the technology. He had spun out a commercial company, but he didn't have any money, any management, any marketing, or any sales. We had everything he didn't—but he had what we didn't: He had an installed base."

Carol had succeeded in raising venture capital for her company, so she had plenty of money in the bank. She knew she could probably outspend her competitor, but it would take time. Instead of fighting him, she thought it might make more sense to join forces.

"So I literally cold-called him and said, "Let's talk about what we are doing." We got together and found we had really complimentary skills. This was in those early days when you could just sit around a table and figure out what the deal would cost and then just do it!"

Carol decided to buy her competitor and put the two companies together. In making that decision, she tempted fate. Mergers and acquisitions may be the sexiest business stories in the financial pages, but they mostly don't work. Depending on whose research you credit, 50 to 80 percent of deals fail. The contracts get signed and the bankers get paid, but then the economies of scale, which the combination of companies were supposed to produce, prove elusive. Corporate cultures and computer systems don't mesh. Business turbulence, challenging in any event, prove too much for the fragile, newly combined company. Teams malfunction as margins for error shrink. Deal frenzy makes everyone overoptimistic at first and then just exhausted. Customers get short shrift from frightened employees who are too worried about their job security to do their jobs at all. The strategic purpose for which the deal was invented in the first place disappears in a puff of smoke. The price of acquisitions usually turns out to be far, far higher than any subsequent value.[1]

Mergers and acquisitions are high-risk ventures—expensive and unlikely to succeed. In addition, they're usually reported as titanic ego struggles of a kind that would make them repellent to women. You'd think that if women conformed to their image of being risk-averse, they'd stay away, but they don't. When they see an opportunity to serve the business through acquisition, they go for it. They just don't get carried away. They approach M & A as cautiously and as carefully as any long-term relationship.

Nothing about the Universal Learning Technology and WebCT deal was simple. ULT was based in Boston; WebCT was in Vancouver. ULT was a VC-backed start-up designed to make money for its investors; WebCT sprang from a nonprofit institution. ULT was run by a saleswoman; WebCT was run by a male academic. Each company had its own nationality, founder, culture, brand, product, and name.

"We did the acquisition in May 1999 and then decided that we could not run parallel products. We had a small installed base with our technology, and WebCT had about six hundred customers. We did one of those market/financial/technology assessments, and the long and the short of it was that WebCT had established a brand with its installed base and its roots in academia. So we decided to rename the whole company WebCT. That was a big issue because I had founded Universal Learning Technology. I had to ask: Is this going to be a problem for me? I was more tied to it than anyone because it was something I had founded."

Carol had confronted the central truth about mergers: They are always intensely emotional—not just for women but for everyone. The fact that mergers fuel such passions is of course why they play out as high drama in national newspapers. These passions are usually neglected in the analysis of M & A and underrated by CEOs who have to make the deals work.

After accepting that her company name needed to be sacrificed, Carol faced an even tougher question: What to do with two competing products in the marketplace?

"I didn't feel as tied to that because I am not a developer,"

Carol conceded. "For me it was just a question of where we would have the most advantage in the market. If we were going to continue to use our own product, BRAVO, it would mean we had to convert all the WebCT users. A lot of cost was implied in that, and we'd be bound to lose some of them. For me it was all about customers: customer comfort, customer loyalty, customer perspective. The product is mission-critical to faculties and departments, and I was worried that they would feel that some big corporation had taken over. I really wanted to minimize that impression—the 'here come the blue suits' sort of thing.

"WebCT already had momentum going. Their brand had been established. Other than for ego purposes, I couldn't see why we should keep our own technology alive. It was a bit more current, but not enough to make that much difference. So I thought: Why not go in the other direction? Why not kill off BRAVO?"

However well considered Carol's decision was, it wasn't one that she took lightly. She may not be a developer herself, but she had a lot of insight into how her own technology team would feel. They had poured long nights, weekends, hopes, and dreams into BRAVO, and it had only just begun to be used.

"A death. There's no question," Carol recalled. She was laughing now, but she wasn't then. "I joke about it, but when you talk about sensitivity . . . There were definitely people who felt bummed about it because their product was being abandoned. We had a whole team that was working for it, and this was their baby. It was born, it was launched, and they had put their heart and soul into it. How are you sensitive to that?"

Many CEOS might have been tempted to explain why what had to be had to be and to move on. The emotion of the situation might have unnerved or repulsed them. But not Carol. Instead of denying or attempting to suppress all the fears and feelings implicit in the situation, she faced them head-on.

"It was a bereavement, and I felt that we had to acknowledge it just as in any death. So we had a memorial service. We literally stood around and had readings about the product, remembered it, had a eulogy! It was kinda fun. We remembered it fondly for what it had done for us and what it had meant for the company. And then it was put into a vault.

"We didn't," she added, laughing, "cremate it."

Having successfully navigated one emotional minefield, Carol still had two separate teams to manage. WebCT's CEO, Murray Goldberg, now reporting to Carol, stayed in Vancouver to look after his engineering team. They were a long way from the Boston headquarters, and they didn't know Carol. They were heartened by the survival of their product and their company name, but they still worried about their new American owner.

"The whole team in Vancouver, it was a total jolt in the arm for them when we kept the name and the product. They were ecstatic. Despite the fact that I said I didn't want the customers to think that the blue suits had arrived, the whole Vancouver group felt that the blue suits *had* arrived! Their greatest fear was that the new company would come in, would shut them down, take their product, rape them, and go away. That was as much of an issue for me as it was for the customers; in fact, it was more of an issue to have this team understand that wasn't what we were doing."

In many companies the existence of two teams in two countries with two leaders would have signaled the beginning of a major turf war, with each side determined to prove the other incompetent, old-fashioned, inferior. In this case, aggressive steps to enforce the dominance of one culture over another would probably have proved catastrophic. But instead of acting as the enforcer, Carol empathized. On her frequent trips to Vancouver, she was always careful to wear jeans and not a suit.

"Most of the people in Vancouver are young. And on top of being young, there is a different mindset with a Canadian employee. It is just different. Forget about just being an acquirer—that would be hard enough. Put 'American' on top of it *and* a VC-backed company! You have to acknowledge that all those thoughts are running through people's minds.

"You can't just say, 'I'm not going to shut you down.' Nobody believes those words. They have to see that, over six months, you don't close them down. I think it was making commitments and following through, over a nine- to twelve-month period, before people settled in and thought, 'They mean what they say. We are here to stay.' I think the cement has to dry over a certain period of time. You just can't walk in and say, 'This is it. Everybody happy? Yup? Good. Done.'"

The cement needs time to dry. The emotions need time to cool off. Carol never tried to ram her merger through. She expected it to require a lot of love and attention, and it did. She knew she'd inherited a culture clash that wouldn't go away unless she took decisive steps to address it. She installed video conferencing equipment so that people could get to know one another's faces. She sent technical teams back and forth regularly, investing time and money in the relationships between the two offices. She said it helped that Boston and Vancouver were both great cities, on the water, and of roughly equivalent size. It was not, she said, like Boston and Podunk. Every year WebCT holds a users' conference, and every year they alternate between locations. She goes to great lengths and expense to ensure that her merger really feels like a merger, that no one feels like the dominated partner.

"Are there inherent problems in it? Absolutely. Three thousand
miles away. Would I rather have everyone in the same building?
Absolutely. Do we have a much cheaper workforce in Vancouver? Absolutely. You saw our Canadian Mountie out in the reception. We have Canadian flags all around the office. It's interesting
because we don't have American flags flying in the Vancouver
office. I've spent more time making the Canadians feel comfortable with the Americans than the other way around."

"Embody the Anxiety" is one of Carol's mantras. Instead of
letting that anxiety fester, she actively seeks ways for it to get out.
While many business textbooks describe business as *un*emotional
and imply that that is how it ought to be, Carol knows that business will always arouse feelings because it involves people.

"You have to assume that this is all happening to a person,
not just a business. When a change happens, people deny it. Then
they get angry and finally accept it. One of my themes is 'This,
too, shall pass.' Another is 'It is what it is.' So we are where we
are right now, and we can spend a lot of time saying, 'Gee, I wish
I had positioned this differently,' but you can't change it. It's a
waste of time. It is what it is, and this, too, shall pass."

It is what it is. What is so striking about Carol's approach is
that she never talks about what *ought* to be, how people *should*
feel. She has no rigid business system into which she is trying to
force her people. Instead, she remains highly responsive to them,
able to respond to the feelings and mood swings inevitable in the
drama of a growing business.

"You are supposed to have the perfect child, but you don't.
And you can't make a child sleep through the night! You can't

make a child behave the way you want him to no matter how much you want him to. It is just not going to work that way. I have to understand what things I can change and what things I can't, and what things I just have to pay attention to.

"From the time that our youngest was very young, we always said, 'This is what is going to happen next.' If he was going to go to the doctor, I would say, 'The shot is going to hurt a little bit. Just know that it is going to hurt a little bit, but it isn't going to be worse than this.' And he was never anxious. He just rolled into the next thing. I feel the same thing with companies. People get anxious if they fear what is coming next, if they are not quite sure. So you have to tell them what you're going to do, and then you have to do it."

Against all the odds, Carol's merger of WebCT and Universal Learning Technology has worked. It has allowed her to build revenues, margins, and market share faster than she could have done alone. A few years later she went on to do another successful acquisition. Because she has been unflinching in her recognition of the tensions, competitiveness, and anxiety inherent in her deals, she has been able to find in herself and in her management team ways of dealing with the maelstrom of feelings that her business decisions provoked.

Carol started her company because she was convinced that technology had a lot to offer education and because she wanted to build a big successful business. She has a strong sense of right and wrong, but I don't think I've ever seen her really angry. By contrast, Wendy Lopez can get mad—but when she does, she puts her feelings to highly productive use. Like many female entrepreneurs, Wendy started her Texas construction firm, Wendy Lopez Associates, because she had something to prove.

"When I first started my business, I did it partly because I was so pissed off about the way people talked about women- and minority-owned firms. 'There's no one any good out there,' they'd say. 'If I have to use them, I'd pay to keep them off my project.' Part of what made me so mad was that it is just not true. They basically thought that unless you were a white guy, you couldn't do good work."

Wendy was determined to show that she could do work much better than that. "My whole focus was on delivering high-quality services that would exceed expectations. We always tried to give our clients a little bit extra, to build in that wow factor so that the next time they'd remember what we did for them and ask us to do more."

Wendy Lopez Associates opened for business in Dallas in 1997, doing structural engineering work on big transportation and environmental projects. Because it was both woman- and minority-owned, the company qualified for government Empowerment Contracting Programs, but it soon became clear that clients stayed with Wendy Lopez Associates because there was nothing she would not do for them.

"If they wanted me to count power poles, I'd do it. No job was too small or menial. I'd develop a database and a map to find those poles. If they hired a big firm, they'd never have gotten serious attention—just a young guy who may or may not do a good job. But nothing would go out of our office that wasn't perfect. It's just the way I am."

Within five years the firm had 170 employees. It was too big to be considered a small business anymore and no longer qualified for minority or small business status.

"It's always been my philosophy," said Wendy, "that if you are crossing some big milestone, don't just cross—get some momentum and leap! I thought we'd survive better if we were a lot stronger, offering more services and more people. I didn't just want to be a big small business."

For years Wendy had been aware of a competitor in Fort Worth. Everyone she knew kept telling her, "You need to meet Rudy Garcia. He does the same stuff you do."

"He was hearing the same thing about me. So finally we met one day, and we developed a mutual friendship and respect. We'd get together about once a year and have dinner and talk about our companies and what we were planning even though we were competitors—because we had each built one of the most successful minority companies in the public sector in the Dallas/Fort Worth area."

Although they'd gone into business within about two months of each other, Wendy's was by now the bigger firm. She thinks it was she who first broached the idea of a merger; Rudy thinks it was his idea. They were both thinking along the same lines, but in October 2000, Rudy wasn't quite ready to make the leap.

"He could appreciate what I was saying about impetus. We were both growing out of the small business programs. We talked more and decided the time wasn't right. I didn't push him." But six months later Rudy called Wendy and said he thought the time had come. They hired a facilitator and sat down to hammer out a merger agreement. Because Wendy Lopez Associates was the bigger business, they engineered a 55-45 stock swap. Fixing the price, making the deal, Rudy recalled, was the easy part. The two organizations fitted together well—at least on paper.

"Garcia was stronger in highway design," recalled Wendy, "and we were stronger in environmental services. In some we would take the lead, and vice versa. We traded 55 percent of Garcia for 45 percent of Lopez. Lopez was a bit bigger than Garcia, and it wasn't one of those deals based on balance sheets. You knew you had to do it that way, which guys would probably never do. I was looking more at the future than at the past numbers.

"We thought the news would blow everyone's socks off, and it did! It was a big deal in our industry for the two firms to get together because we had been the poster children in the public sector of companies that had done it the right way, built strong reputations and credentials and resources. But our timing was terrible because 2002 economically was god-awful. We had all these people and all this excitement, and it fizzled because lots of projects got put on hold."

As the economy shrank, the questions started. "Will Rudy and Wendy be able to get along? Dallas and Fort Worth may be only thirty-five miles apart, but they may as well be a thousand! Dallas is fast-paced and cosmopolitan, and Fort Worth is very laid-back. So there's all that cultural stuff. Whose culture was going to dominate?

"Also, we had a lot of overlap, so people worried about who would survive. The biggest thing was for the staff: those who used to report to one boss now had to report to a new boss who didn't know them, didn't know how good they were, didn't know how they liked to work. That was the biggest obstacle—the staff getting used to the change."

Wendy became CEO and focused more on external business, and Rudy became president and focused on operations. It suited them well. Wendy said they were both "happy little clams about it." But the staff remained anxious, worried about their future and often not entirely happy about the way the new organization was structured.

"We lost some people," said Wendy, "but none that I miss. The people who are here went through some difficult times. One, who is COO, is a civil engineer and was absolutely my right-hand person when we were still Wendy Lopez Associates. Suddenly, she was reporting to Rudy, who is very different to work for. He's much more of a deep thinker. If you ask him something, you may have to ask three times, whereas I'll give you an answer before you leave the room. Well, she found this very hard to work with, and I almost lost her. We then revised the org chart so she could report to me. You could say we compromised and caved in, but the truth is I wanted her to be happy and I made the changes necessary to make that happen. I wasn't so stubborn that I dug my heels in. But I did what was best for the firm."

Because she was determined to keep her best people, on the grounds that that had to be best for the firm, Wendy wasn't rigid, or doctrinaire. She and Rudy worked it all out on paper, but there were still a lot of adjustments to be made in real life.

"Today, Rudy and I both do inside and outside stuff. It's not as clear-cut as we thought it would be. It has evolved, and we didn't get in the way of the evolution. If something didn't work, we'd tweak it and get it to work better. We listened a lot and continue to listen.

"Did I ever doubt myself? Oh, yes. Especially when I was tired and was working as hard as I could and was doing everything I could think of to make it better—and it was still tanking! No matter what you try, it can still suck. There are periods when everything you do just doesn't seem to work. And it felt like that for three years. And then there are other times (we're in one right now) when everything is great. We just won an $8 million contract and we are on a roll, and it doesn't matter if you screw up little things. You have to enjoy the good times and outlast the bad because the good will come again."

Given the opportunity, Wendy and Rudy are both eager to

sing each other's praises, but they're very different people. Wendy is vivacious, fast-talking, and effervescent. Rudy Garcia is thoughtful, soft-spoken, and reflective. He recalled this transition period more calmly than Wendy did, but it's clear that it was tough for both of them.

"It's just like a marriage," Rudy reflected. "You have to get used to the way other people do things. I think what made our company more successful is that Wendy and I have learned to talk to each other. We had to do that. It never stops. And, just like a marriage, if you don't speak up, it's your fault. It's your company."

So what is it that allowed Carol and Wendy and their two mergers to succeed where so many have failed? In both cases the mergers were followed by periods of profound market turbulence—a cause often cited for M & A failure. And yet both of these business leaders, with a new business under their wings, managed to ride out that turbulence and emerge with stronger businesses. How did they do it?

You might say that they succeeded because they were relatively small, but I've known (and done) smaller deals that proved impossible to succeed. Indeed, in small firms the emotions are often so much more intense that they're harder to make work than those that are bigger and have more established processes. Big deals are often wrecked by their complexity, it's true, but it doesn't follow that smaller transactions are simple. Clearly, in both cases the CEOs chose well. They found business partners who weren't threatened by their stronger positions—in Carol's case, the fact that she had more investment dollars; in Wendy's case, the fact that she owned the larger firm. In both cases, there was absolute clarity about who would become CEO. There was none of the mealy-mouthed, partnership-of-equals equivocation that salves egos but confuses the workforce.

Neither CEO ever delegated responsibility for the merger; indeed, it was almost the opposite. Both felt that their own success was highly contingent on the merger's success. They felt personally implicated in their deals and responsible for everything that flowed from it. They didn't sign the paperwork and then throw it over a wall for integration teams to figure out. They stayed with it for as long as it took. And it took a long time. As Carol Vallone said, you have to let the cement dry. Between the time that she first had the idea and the time the deal was done, Wendy Lopez was prepared to wait a full year. Carol didn't just pontificate about her strategy; she gave her Canadian team time to believe that it was real and credible. Both women stayed continuously mindful of the ripples that their deals made; their vigilance and patience paid off.

Some business texts would regard this as indulgent, undisciplined, but I think one characteristic of both deals is that they were highly realistic about the time, money, and emotions that were in play. Neither CEO expected her merger to generate miracles; neither ever conceived of some kind of "magic bullet" or was driven by a desire to impress the market. Both mergers made operational as well as strategic sense.

And, finally, neither CEO approached her merger with a formulaic, rules-driven preconception about how it ought to play out. Neither tried to squeeze the companies into a mold that didn't fit. Some might regard this as woolly, undisciplined, and unstructured, but I think they'd be wrong. By remaining alert to the shifting moods and mind-sets of their companies and cultures, both CEOs were able to keep the businesses productive and focused on the future. They never dodged the hard, emotional issues that surfaced, nor did they attempt to persuade their workforce to suppress them. What stands out in these stories is how unafraid of emotions these women were. They know that business is, always has been, and always will be emotional. It absorbs the most precious, irreplaceable thing we have: time. How could it not be emotional? It is only by embracing and understanding the power of emotion in business that these women became so adept at managing it.

13. Birth of a Saleswoman

Selling your business represents one kind of success. It means you have succeeded on your own terms in building an asset. It is—or should be—a triumph. But selling also means letting go forever. The most frequent reference used to articulate the passionate engagement women have with their companies is that of a mother and child. It is time to walk away, to see if that child can stand on its own two feet—and see if the mother can, too. The ultimate test of a company and its founder may be whether they can thrive apart.

Concluding a successful merger didn't mean plain sailing for WebCT afterward. They had launched as a software company, but as the market embraced e-commerce, they changed their business model.

"The concept was this: The students are using this application, on average, one and a half to two hours a day. They are hitting up against a resource site all the time, so the resource site is where we are getting the eyeballs and where we are putting advertising. We could charge very little for the application and get our value out of the ads." Carol Vallone laughs as she remembers those early days. "What was different for us was the fact that we had the base. A lot of companies were trying to buy the base, but we had it. Millions of students! We were sort of in this nirvana position."

So perfect did WebCT's position look that the company began to ready itself for an IPO, but then the market crashed. All bets were off. Some of her investors wanted Carol to cut costs and get to profitability as fast as possible. This she refused to do. Other investors urged her to keep growing the business. Their voices, and Carol's, won the day. And so the company became an enterprise software company again.

"Every year we had that same tension. Our strategic investors wanted us to keep growing. Our financial investors wanted us to cut to profitability. We rode through the middle of that, and our growth rate and successes were positive through that period. We went from $2 million to $5 million to $10 million to $20 million to $30 million. So when you say you are going to transition and your revenues do that growth curve, you get very excited. It is market acceptance of what you are doing."

Success like this could not go unnoticed, and one day WebCT's arch competitor, Blackboard, called Carol. It was a tricky moment. Heretofore, Carol, the arch saleswoman, had always demonized Blackboard. "They came to us with an unsolicited offer. I said I really wasn't interested."

But Carol couldn't just turn her back on the offer, so she did what she always did: She sat down and analyzed the alternatives. Could they do an IPO on their own? She didn't think the business had the right scale yet. Could they achieve that scale through more mergers? She wasn't convinced the M & A market held enough opportunities for her. Could they just keep growing? Yes, they could, but her investors had been in for a long time now. She then hired Goldman Sachs to look at other options.

"The long and the short of the story is we discussed it with the board, and they said to see how good a deal we could get. Well, my indifference just made the deal get better and better. It went on for months. And then we got it to be four times revenue, all cash. So how do you walk away? It was over a number of months. I had a huge number of sleepless nights and ultimately decided. If we sold, everyone got money back plus some. It was time to do a deal at a great multiple and move on. It was full of mixed emotions, but I thought I had to do what was right for our shareholders."

Most business owners don't have an exit strategy.[1] Many are just too busy to think about it; some don't want to think about it. But if the company is successful, sooner or later it has to be considered. Her business is usually the most valuable asset a businesswoman has, so the question inevitably arises: What is the best way to realize or extract that value? Some, like Carol Vallone, think about and approach a public offering. Some, like Carol Latham, think about handing the business on to their children. About half of all women business owners expect to sell all or part of their businesses one day, and there are as many ways to do so as there are companies.[2] Some owners use investment bankers, some don't. Some seek strategic investors, hoping to exit gradually, while others prefer a quick, total break. What is true across the board is that everyone finds the transition emotional.

"What made it worse," said Carol Vallone, "was not being able to tell the employees. We told them that we were working with Goldman, but we didn't tell them every day what companies we were talking to. You don't want them churning, so *you* have to do the churning. Not talking about it was like 'oh my god!' You are living in a dual existence and it's not my style to do that."

Carol had lots of concerns. What would a sale mean for her employees? What would it mean for the culture she had created? What would it mean for her customers? In this, she was not unusual. Research into exit strategies has shown that while men and women are equally concerned about getting a good price when selling their businesses, women owners are significantly more likely than men owners to take into account the future well-being of their businesses and their employees.[3]

"I kept thinking: What are my objections, and can I get over them and feel comfortable? I had demonized Blackboard. Culturally, we don't run business the same way. Legally, I knew I had to consider that my first responsibility was to my shareholders. I was very concerned about my customers and the employees, so we did a ton of the work at the front end, laying out and dealing with all the issues I was uncomfortable with. We produced a twelve-page document about how the employees, the shareholders, and the customers would be treated and communicated with. When we finally made the announcement, we had answers to all their concerns. You don't want to be making it up. You want a joint commitment. Things like that were important to me."

Carol didn't rush. The thought of the money she'd make didn't make her giddy. She recognized that, as she said, "once you're gone, you're gone." She structured the deal to protect employees and customers as well as she could. And because Blackboard was a publicly traded company, she knew that if they didn't honor their commitments, they'd lose the employees and the customers they had paid so much for. So she was relying on a contract but also on mutual self-interest to protect the people and the values she cared about.

"Blackboard has been highly sensitized to our issues, but in the end they'll do what they want to do. In the academic part of the business, half the employees will be ours. If we can't impact the culture with those numbers, then shame on us."

As you might expect, she put a lot of time, attention, and resources into communicating the deal to the company. "We hired outside consultants to advise us on how to work with employees and how to make an announcement. We have been rigorous and religious about meeting with employees. We have communications every week. We've done myriads of phone meetings and intranets. We have given everyone so much information because otherwise they'll make up their own. There's a lot of natural anxiety in any transition, and you have to replace that anxiety with information. So now I feel like people's heads are in the right place."

Employees were anxious, of course, but they also recognized at this turning point just how much they'd gained from the experience of being part of WebCT.

"One of the things I have been rewarded by is how many people have said to me, 'I have never worked at a better place in terms of culture and making one another successful, instead of stepping over each other for personal success.' Many men came forward on this topic—females have always been appreciative—but senior executive men came up to tell me how nice it was to work in a place without bullshit and backstabbing. And their opinion was that it came from the top."

What Carol tried hard to do (and only time will tell how successful she has been) was look after everyone: investors, employees, and customers. She used everything she could think of to protect their interests. What she didn't think about very much was herself.

"What does this mean for me? No idea. It was so hectic trying to get a deal closed. I couldn't think straight. I couldn't even breathe. I just couldn't think about it."

MOVING SWIFTLY ON

On the Friday before Labor Day 2002, at 3:40 P.M., Lurita Doan was walking out the door to start the weekend a little early when the phone rang. It was the United States Customs Office (now part of the Department of Homeland Security), and they had a problem. President Bush was going to Detroit on Tuesday to talk to Jean Chrétien, the prime minister of Canada, about the Smart Border Initiative—a government strategy to deploy technology for national border security. But there wasn't any surveillance technology on the Ambassador Bridge where the two heads of state were due to meet. Could NTMI install some over the weekend so that the president would have something to show the Canadians on Tuesday?

"We said we would love to. I mean, sure, all the stuff on the Canadian side had to be done in French, and it was the Labor Day weekend. We'd had no notice at all, but of course we did it. We rented helicopters to install cameras on bridges. We found every French speaker in the company we could! One of the guys was so excited, he taped an NTMI business card to the bridge before he came home. It was quite something. I found out later that they'd called all the big companies first—Lockheed Martin, Cisco—but they couldn't do it in time."

Lurita Doan's decision to focus on surveillance paid off, and the company's growth was fueled by successes like this one. By 2004, NTMI had over 250 employees and revenues in the region of $210 million. Along the way, many people had recommended that Lurita take advantage of her phenomenal growth and bring more investment into the business.

"We were always getting calls to do an IPO or to get a strategic investor, take venture capital. Everyone kept saying to me:

'It's time for you to take a little bit off the table.' But I'd say, 'Don't you understand? I'm a southern woman. I *like* a laden table! I want it to be available for everyone.'

"Strategic investors are great, everyone said. You've earned it. You'll feel safer. But there's no way that I want to own a little of something. I like to have my way. He who pays the piper . . . Okay, so I take strategic investment. Maybe he wouldn't be first fiddle, but he'd be second fiddle. And I wouldn't be able to make decisions as fast.

"Then everyone said I should do an IPO, but I felt I wasn't ready. My neighbor did one, and he was on a plane for six months and then got divorced! I looked at that and at everyone I knew, and I just thought it was the wrong thing to do."

But as NTMI and its profile grew, so did Lurita's, and she was approached for a presidential appointment.

"It was a strange thing. I had been approached for a position, not at cabinet level but nearly, and it was perfect. It was one of my life's ambitions. But I couldn't do that and keep my business, so it was really the most compelling reason to sell. It's hard to give up one thing when you don't have something else. A year ago I could never have imagined giving up my business—but only because there was no incentive. Now there was an incentive."

Once the idea was planted in her mind, it grew. The idea of doing something else. The idea that the company could live without her and even flourish without her. She started thinking about the qualities that a different owner might be able to bring to the company. In other words, Lurita started to separate mentally from her "baby." She started to think about the kind of buyer that would be bearable.

"I was looking for people who didn't want to cannibalize the company. If we had been bought by competitors, they'd have chopped up the divisions, and people would never have worked together again. In our company, teams are really important, and they trust one another. If you cannibalize that, it wouldn't work effectively. It was also important to sell to someone who would respect salaries and all the fringe benefits we provide because we provide so many."

Lurita also thought long and hard about herself, about how she would feel most comfortable walking away.

"I knew I didn't want to keep any ownership at all. Usually people do an earn out, but I wanted a clean break. I don't know how not to be in charge of something. I don't know how not to give 150 percent, and I don't know how to give up on something. In any sale the employees have to buy into the new regime; it's like a new marriage. They have to bind themselves to the new owners, and as long as I was around, there would always be some employees who would look to me.

"I didn't have a broker. Everyone says you should never do that, but I figured I was good with numbers and know industry standards and the value of my business. I know what I am willing to put up with and what I'm not. I thought I needed a good accountant and a good mergers and acquisitions lawyer, so I got them. We wrote the contract and told people: If you are interested, say so. If not, fine. The first buyer said yes."

With characteristic speed and decisiveness, Lurita assembled a small team to do the deal in just under a month. She involved only a few colleagues—the CFO, COO, her own assistant, and her director of operations. And she worked hard to make sure that the new owners would encounter no surprises.

"It is so funny. Our company has lots of good things, and it also has some warts. To me the simplest thing was to explain both. I think the new owners kept thinking there was some hidden agenda behind this, but I just wanted to be sure that they knew everything. The other thing that surprised me was how much people focused on pennies. I refused to haggle over pennies. For example, there was a lot of cash in the business, and they kept calling to make sure I hadn't written a big fat check to myself. I kept explaining that I was leaving that cash in the business because operating funds are needed. Of course I'm not going to write myself a check the night before the transaction closes!"

The deal closed at 3:00 P.M. and was announced an hour and a half later to all employees.

"Every single employee took the time to write me a note, send me an e-mail, or stop by to see me in person to thank me for hiring them and to wish me well. The sheer number of thank-you and going away parties was actually embarrassing, not to mention the quantity of flowers I received and two very special bracelets."

Lurita did agree to stay on, but only for a very short period. For sixty days after the sale "I helped to transition the new owners and the new CEO they put in my place. During that time I tried to be the best employee NTMI ever had. I worked, on average, about twelve hours each day, Monday through Saturday, even though my transition employment contract specified only fifty hours per week. I also wrote three proposals for contracts valued at approximately $40 million. I took approximately fifty folders that had my ideas for upcoming opportunities and wrote notes on each one, detailing my thoughts about the idea, what the new owners might need to do, and who at NTMI would be the best people to continue or to consult with regarding the opportunity. I figure I did about one-third of a man-year in the sixty-day period."

Lurita doesn't expect the company to stay the same. "The culture will not stay the same, and it should not," she said. "That would be very wrong. The new owners say they want to run it just like me, but I told them I thought that was wrong. I didn't do everything right! They should keep the things that are right, such as the teams, the trust, the way we do things on spec, with lots of innovation. But some of the bad things (for example, we don't fire people fast enough) should be changed. You have to put your own stamp on things, make people see that there is a difference but a good difference. Sure, I'd like things to stay the same—like the fact that it isn't hierarchical and everyone gets a say. But I would be disappointed if, in two years' time, it looked the same as the day I left."

The presidential appointment took longer than expected to come through; at times Lurita wondered if it would happen at all. It was hard for her not to know what would happen next. "My husband begged me not to start another business for six months," said Lurita, "and I promised I wouldn't. My job right now is to learn how to do nothing. But I am so glad that I sold the company. After fifteen years I think the time was right, both because my interests have changed to a more global focus and also because I do not know how to give less than everything to a task. So I am happy to have this time to refresh myself for the next phase of my life—whatever that new involvement might ultimately become. I believe the new owners were a good match, and I have enormous respect for the man they put in to serve as the new president and CEO. I would be worried for NTMI's future if they had put a less capable executive in the slot, but I think NTMI is in excellent hands."

Although she felt comfortable with her decisions, the transition out of NTMI was tough on Lurita. Looking at colleges for her daughter was important, but nothing matched the excitement that came into her voice when she talked about her business. Finally, after waiting nearly a year, Lurita was nominated by the president for the post of administrator of General Services. As she prepared to move on, she recognized that it was inevitable and even desirable for the company also to move on to its next growth phase. Both she and Carol Vallone got themselves out of the way fast, as if they knew that sticking around might prove too painful. It is a lesson everyone at Thermagon has had to learn the hard way.

IN MOURNING

"I have two sons in the business," said Carol Latham. "And for a while I really thought I had the cat by the tail. But when we went through the downturn in 2002, I became concerned about what would have happened if I had not been there. My eldest son kind of folded. I have invested my whole life in this. It didn't matter who I'd hire to come in and run the company—I wasn't going to be happy with that scenario. So I knew that I needed to sell the business."

Carol is sixty-six. If she had contemplated handing the company on to her sons, the downturn persuaded her otherwise. So now she had to figure out how to realize the value of what she'd built.

"During the whole life of the business I'd had suitors. There were always people knocking on the door and asking if they could buy. My experience with large companies like BP wasn't positive. Companies like 3M, GE, or ICI could have been a fit in the sense that they're in our space, but I wasn't positive about these companies. They were just too big. I wanted a strategic buyer who was interested in developing the business to the next level.

"I knew that most purchases aren't successful, so I was really concerned. First of all, we had a culture here that was unique. These people were like an extension of my family. I was very concerned about what would happen to them. Second, there were all the external people, such as my Taiwanese friend and others around the world who were our channel to market. What would happen to those people who had supported us?"

Determined that a large company would not treat Thermagon with the care it needed, Carol looked at midsized companies in her market.

"Laird had chased me for four years. It was a medium-sized company, and that intrigued me. The chairman announced that he was going to be in the thermal business. They'd bought a couple of smaller companies in the same sort of area. It was definitely a strategic fit."

The Laird Group is a United Kingdom–based conglomerate that has been built by acquisition. It specializes in thermal materials and wireless antennae needed by high-tech electronics manufacturers. It is run entirely by men, and it doesn't have a single woman director on its board. But Carol couldn't find any companies that were a good cultural fit, so she decided to sell to Laird. She was sufficiently uncomfortable with the deal, however, that she decided to commit to a two-year earn-out. She hoped that by staying engaged in the business, she'd be able to protect the people and the culture. But she hasn't been.

"I went to Texas for a business trip, and when I got in one night, I discovered our COO was gone. Not one soul knew. The way it was done, it was just management by fear. They had rated everyone, but they didn't know them. I managed to save two people, but they said they had to cut five. They said, 'This part of the business is a little overweighted.' When people are let go, it's a total surprise. One day the person is gone. They say it is just a matter of numbers. I asked questions but got very unsatisfactory answers. I am just a figurehead now."

Carol's sons, Jim and Craig, are steady, gentle people. They both thought their mother was crazy when she started the business, but they have worked hard for her and have become immensely proud of what she has achieved. Like all the Thermagon employees, they've made money from the sale. They appreciate that Laird may be better positioned to help the company grow and want to be part of that, but they're unnerved by the cultural changes around them and in mourning for the company that Thermagon once was. Both sons acknowledge that their mother has a stronger stomach for change than they do.

"Here, people always came first," recalled Craig. "That included the customers. So we've always been caring, understanding, and compassionate. Where does that come from? Mom was driven to answer customer needs. That wore off on me, and I wanted to do the same for people inside the company, too. And now making numbers is the number one thing, and our customers are suffering."

"Laird told us we had to ship everything for July in June and not to pay our vendors on time," said Jim. "So now we've pissed off everyone. We've pissed off the customers because we've delivered when it wasn't convenient, and we've pissed off our vendors because we haven't paid them on time. And all because it's a public company and we have to hit our numbers. It's really demoralizing not to do the best job you can.

"Was it the right decision to sell? I don't know. My mom does everything on intuition. She founded this company on intuition. She's often right-on."

Carol Latham isn't happy about these developments, but she proved before that she is capable of making tough decisions. "I know how to deal with adversity and out of it comes opportunity. I was divorced and I was a single parent before the phrase was even invented. I walked out of BP with nowhere to hang my hat. So I've been able to master change. Laird is very global and has positioned itself in China, and I think we will end up making some of our products there. In some cases it makes sense because our customers are there, but they also have a big plant in Europe and we have manufacturing there. If the business goes the way it should, they'll all be necessary.

"We were very high end. Laird is about volume. They're developing the lower end of the market. It's like going from Nieman Marcus to Wal-Mart. Price is more of a driver there, and that's a challenge. It's been interesting. I try hard not to get in the way and be as helpful as possible, so I'm cautiously optimistic about how it will go."

Carol is and has always been a visionary, and she wants to see her ideas win. When she built her company, she had one goal: to bring a product to market and have its value recognized. She has achieved that. But she also achieved something unexpected, which was the culture and worth of the company to each employee in it. This, she said, was a total surprise.

Both achievements remain intact. Her technology is becoming ubiquitous. And although Carol feels a deep sense of loss at the changes in company culture, nothing Laird does can take away from her employees the skills, experience, and confidence that her company made possible for them. The company will and must change, but no one and nothing can touch all that Carol gave to those who built it with her. Whatever happens next to Jim or Craig or Mistelina Quinones or the other Thermagon employees, their lives have been vastly enriched by the value that Carol Latham created out of nothing.

STAYING ON

In the summer of 2005, Beth Bronfman was approached by a competitor who was interested in buying her advertising agency. She was definitely interested.

"This is a discussion point now. I am fifty-four and my partner is sixty-three, but he will never retire. The truth is, you have to think of a succession plan ten years in advance if you're going to have the choices you want to have. We have a lot of young blood here, and I love what I do. The people are important to me, and the culture is important to me. But I have to think about the future."

As she discussed the prospect of selling her company, Beth was clearly torn. She is passionate about her people, her employees, and her clients. She cherishes her freedom to decide employee bonuses. She adores the personal relationship she has enjoyed for years with her clients. She's a high-energy, action-oriented woman who wants to do the right thing.

"We could buy someone. Merge. Grow as fast as we can now so we're worth more later. What are we going to do? I don't know what I'm going to do."

Although when talking to her it really does seem that Beth *could* go on forever, she won't. But she'd like her business to. After twenty years, her agency is well known and well respected. So when one of the big three ad agencies in New York—she calls them "the big boys"—expressed an interest in buying it, on one level she was flattered. It was an accolade. It proved her achievement. She was interested.

"We're a straightforward, traditional, creative ad agency. We don't do ancillary marketing such as special events or PR except when the client absolutely needs us. I'd always thought the big conglomerates wanted the ancillary businesses, so I was very surprised. It proved that a company like ours can do great because we are very entrepreneurial and are very close to our clients. The big guys aren't as resilient and resourceful, so they have a need."

Beth's lawyer suggested that the company conduct a bake sale—that is, see if they could create a bidding war to force the company's price up. But Beth wasn't willing to go that far that fast. The company that had approached her asked for numbers and a confidentiality agreement, and they hadn't even met yet.

"Our numbers were fine in terms of what they were looking for, but I explained that I wanted to meet. I wanted to have a first date before handing over the numbers. So we met with them, and it went great. We went through best- and worst-case scenarios. We talked about our lease and whether we'd work in their space or ours. They liked us. They knew we could make money, and they said they could show us how to make more money.

"Now, when our agency says we'll do an ad for a client, we give them a price and we stick to it. We will do whatever it takes to do the very best ad for that price. That's why we keep our clients *and* our creatives forever. But they said, 'This is a business, and after a while you have to cut off the work.' But my creatives *love* knowing that they can do the best product they can dream up, with no restrictions. That's how we kept growing!

"One of the other things they said was 'You won't keep being pestered by people asking for raises all the time because we have a corporate policy that people get bonuses and raises just once a year. That's it.' But in my company we give bonuses every time we win a new client. That's how we keep people. We look after them, and they look after us.

"I realized that the way I run this organization is right for me. We are very profitable and keep growing, but we don't decide everything by numbers. We're flexible, but when you're a big corporation, that can't be the way you do things. I was beginning to feel that this sale wasn't right for me and for the culture I'd created."

Beth didn't have a bake sale, and she didn't sell the company. She's still thinking about whether to buy something herself or merge with another company. She'll always be thinking about it, but for now she knows that she likes the way her company runs and she doesn't want to see its values change.

GROWING UP

Since I began writing this book, Adrian Guglielmo sold Diversity Partners and Irene Cohen sold FlexCorp. The rest of the companies haven't reached that crossroads yet. At Trade Settlement, Pat Loret de Mola has been approached by three corporate suitors who would like to acquire the company but she's decided to partner with them instead—at least for now. Those partnerships will propel expansion into Europe. In the meantime, Pat is also increasing the company's product offerings so that she can expand both what she sells and where she sells it. This will, of course, just make the company more valuable. At Andavo Travel, Brenda Rivers now knows that her daughter doesn't want to inherit the business and, to realize its value, she will have to sell it. She is just starting to look for potential acquirers but with sales growing "by leaps and bounds," she isn't in a hurry. At Delaire, Lori Hallock would love to pass the company on to her daughter but she worries about when she'll be ready and how much control she can have over timing. In the meantime, their sales are soaring and they're about to expand into a new building. Nadine Lange, at Open Scan, has been approached by three different companies to discuss acquisition. She isn't sure it's time yet. She's still having fun, revenues are up 50 percent in one year, and they are still developing new products.

At Eileen Fisher, the company is just beginning to roll out an Employee Stock Option Plan. In effect, Eileen will give 30 percent of her company to her employees, making them all shareholders. This is in addition to an existing profit sharing scheme, 401K plan, and other benefits. Eileen belives that the ESOP gives all employees yet more reason to think and act together for the benefit of the business; it is entirely consistent with company values.

Employee ownership is something Cecilia McCloy at ISSI and Maureen Beal at National Van Lines are thinking about, too. Both companies continue to grow by nurturing and developing their employees. At National Van Lines, Maureen has received numerous honors from her industry and from her local community. But she is most delighted by the fact that two of National's drivers were awarded the industry's top honor: Super Van Operator of the Year. Out of a field of 167 candidates, only four such awards were given—and two of those went to National drivers.

The Pohly Company, the Eliassen Group, Cenergy, Oxygen, Otis Technology, Edison Automation, Frieda's, Jean's Creams, and Mavens & Moguls are still growing and will be for some years to come. LopezGarcia, as its merger starts to bed down, is seeing high morale and even higher margins. Neutral Posture, having pulled itself back from public ownership, is content now to grow on its own terms and on its own revenues.

Every six months Danlee Medical Supplies receives an offer to buy the business and every six months (so far) Joni Walton has turned it down. Like Beth Bronfman, she still wants to grow her business and to find out how much more she has to give it. At some point all of these owners will face the same issues that Carol Vallone, Lurita Doan, and Carol Latham have faced: whether to stay or go, how to sell, to whom and under what conditions. They will have to know what they want.

"There is one wonderful entrepreneur I know," said banker Nancy Peretsman. "She does not want to have built her company and have it ruined. She is obsessed by where her baby goes—and that's how she thinks about it. The consequence of that is that she will take less money to make sure that the buyer of her company will continue nurturing and protecting and developing the product.

"The key to these things is to understand what you want. It's like saying, 'I want to pay the least rent and have the best address and the best view in New York City.' You can't get all those things together; it's always going to be a question of trade-offs. If you want to stipulate that the company can never merge with another company, you can do that. But that means the buyer may not be able to realize certain cost savings, so the company is worth less. I have had plenty of clients who've said, 'How wonderful to have sold to such-and-such a company,' but you have to know what you want. We spent a lot of time forcing that out; it takes a lot of psychology. But if you come in here and say you want the highest price for your business, you have to accept that there are going to be changes."

Women aren't afraid of change. Even after generations of family ownership, they put the long-term interests of their business first. In 2005, Lauri Union sold a majority stake in her Union Corrugating Company to Chicago Growth Partners, a private equity company. "The company was getting bigger, and I thought that an outside influence would help the company. They'd bring more experience into the business. It meant we would have an outside board, outside ideas. I thought that would be really good for the business." She stayed on as CEO for a while and then moved to a board position, but the company is no longer a family business. "It is a good thing for the company. I don't know if it is good for me as a business person, but it is certainly a good thing for the company." Like all the women business owners in this book, Lauri has put the company's best interests before her own, and she has voted for growth.

Doris Christopher's Pampered Chef hired Goldman Sachs to help her figure out a succession plan. Like Carol Vallone, she considered a public offering but then she sold the business to Warren Buffett's Berkshire Hathaway. What did Buffett like about the business? Its growth rate, its margins, its lack of debt, and its continued growth rate.

The two largest companies in this book, Geraldine Laybourne's Oxygen Network and Carmen Castillo's SDI, may yet go public or be acquired. What's clear is that their growth rate, their demonstrable ability to deliver on expectations, and their dedication to delighting their customers makes them highly attractive investments. What is less clear is when their founders will be willing to let them go.

Because money is only one part of the value that they see in what they've built, selling the business is tough for women. Although the money is a reward, it is really the last reward and only a partial reflection of what has been achieved. Selling is also tough because a big part of the company *is* the founder: her passion, her values, her drive. That changes when the company is sold. But it has to change, as Lurita Doan knows, so that the company can continue to develop.

And the life of the founder has to change, too. Some may go

on to found new companies. Talk to Carol Latham about her new battery technology business, Boston-Power, and you see someone who is eager to tackle a new, difficult problem. Others may go on to be board members, teachers, or advisors, inspiring other women to follow in their wake. It is impossible to imagine any of these women standing still or retiring to a golf course.

All of them have succeeded on their own terms. They set out to prove something and they proved it. They proved, as Geraldine Laybourne said, that the muscle man theory of business is not the only way to succeed. They proved that they could work in their own way, their values intact, and build big, successful, sustainable businesses. Some set out deliberately to change the business world. Others scarcely noticed that that's what they were doing. But these companies, in a myriad of perceptible and imperceptible ways, changed the lives of those who've worked for them, changed the expectations of those who've done business with them, and changed the way that business itself is done. For their owners, the knowledge of these accomplishments is perhaps the greatest reward, richer and deeper than money.

"The great thing about more and more women building and running businesses," said Nancy Peretsman, "is that over time the more attractive part of what you see of behavioral elements may make the whole business community swing to that norm. The great thing is that women *change* the norm. That's an optimistic thought."

14. The New Norm

A few years ago I addressed the partners' meeting at a major investment bank; the subject was men and women at work. I spoke about how the workplace was changing and how men were beginning to follow women in their demand for more flexibility in the way work gets done. Knowing my audience, I filled my talk with data about shifting demographics and workforce attitudes and challenged my audience to think about how their firm would compete. At the end of the session, the first question startled me.

"So what do you do with employees who don't deliver?"

I thought it was a rather irrelevant question, but I answered it anyway: "You ask yourself if the person is in the right position and is being effectively managed. You go through performance reviews and if, after all that, the individual still can't deliver, then he or she has to be fired." I'd done it often. My reply seemed obvious, so banal that I was surprised to find myself spelling it out. Later that day a senior partner gave me some useful feedback.

"You know that stuff you said about the people you've fired? You should put that at the beginning. Nobody here will listen to you until you've proved how tough you can be."

It was good advice because I was in an environment that prized toughness and where all-nighters were a rite of passage, where work was measured in hours, where character was measured in aggression, and where firing people earned respect. I have worked in such environments for years. It has never stopped being alien.

The immense growth and outstanding performance of women-owned businesses offer a profound counterpoint to that mentality. We have always been told that aggression, single-mindedness, lack of feeling, and hard-edged analytical skills were the key requisites for business success, but here we find something different: Smart women with lives, empathy, and imagination who succeed not by aping men but by being themselves. And it isn't a trade-off. They don't tolerate second-rate business results as the cost of their indulgence. They celebrate first-rate business growth *because* they stick to their principles. It is their success that represents a shining challenge to much conventional business wisdom. It demonstrates that there's nothing inevitable or inevitably masculine about the way businesses succeed.

Discovering just how different women's businesses are and why has made me very uncomfortable. When I describe these CEOs as nurturing, it makes me flinch. I did not grow up in an environment in which my female qualities were regarded as anything other than an obstacle in business. I spent a good deal of my career trying to ignore them. So it is a shock to see them as an asset, but it is a very important lesson for the business world as a whole.

It is critical for both men and women to appreciate just how relevant, effective, and successful women's ways of working are, so that everyone will gain confidence in us just the way we are. As relative newcomers to the business environment, we have often been judged—and have judged ourselves—by how well we accommodate ourselves to male norms. It is the wrong yardstick.

The growing success of women-owned businesses demonstrates just how well we can do when we work and lead on our own terms and in our own way, driven by our own vision.

It is essential, too, that established, traditional corporations recognize the achievements of female entrepreneurs. This is the kind of talent those corporations lose every day. Instead of shrugging off such losses with the consolation that "she couldn't cut it," these companies need to ask themselves how they've failed their female talent. What is it about their cultures, about their work habits, that renders them intolerable to precisely the kind of entrepreneurial drive and imagination they know they need? The success of these women should shatter forever the ossified belief that you can't have a family and be fully committed to a professional career. Almost all the women in this book have families, and all make significant commitments to their communities—and yet look at how their companies thrive. It is not despite these relationships but because of them. How long will it take before companies give up the fight for undivided attention and learn to value the external lives and commitments of emotionally rich employees? When will they learn that work and life are not polarized but synthesized?

It is also essential that financial institutions look at these businesses and ask themselves what they have been missing. Women receive less in the way of SBA loans, institutional loans, and venture capital. Yet, even with these cards stacked against them, they're doing very well. Can you imagine what more they might achieve if there was a more level playing field?

It is essential that such customers as federal and state governments and Fortune 500 companies look at these businesses, at their quality, ethics, and sustainability, and ask: Why aren't we doing business with these companies? Given their commitment to their customers and their passion to outperform, shouldn't they be ideal vendors? Can any government or company seriously argue that it delivers the best value to taxpayers and shareholders when it ignores women's businesses?

And last, but definitely not least, it is essential for men to see how effective this female mind-set can be. Why? Because many men don't like the old, macho, command-and-control, dog-eat-dog workplaces, either. No more than their female counterparts do they feel that they should prove themselves by outworking their peers, eschewing their families, and dominating corporate shoot-outs. There are plenty of men out there who would rather work the way that women do and lead the way that women do. I am not convinced that it is their DNA that stops them.

I don't think there is anything in this book that men could not do. The question is when they will be allowed to. For the last fifteen years, business thought leaders have written eloquently about the need for a new kind of leadership: integrated, authentic, whole, human. And most business leaders understand this intellectually. They just find it very hard to do. It is hard to buck the system, to let go of one paradigm before you can firmly grip another. The business-as-war or companies-as-machines metaphors are a long time dying.

But women-owned businesses are now being born and growing at such a prodigious rate that the business landscape itself is starting to change. A few banks are beginning to see that women's companies represent a very good investment. Retailers are starting to see that women bring them both new products and new customers. Professional services firms now appreciate that they won't win new business from female entrepreneurs until they can field female partners to own those accounts.

Every time you do business with someone, it changes you. A

little bit of your customer rubs off. When a woman's company wins a piece of new business, the competitor learns that times are changing. Business is the most interactive relationship in the world, and every day that a new woman-owned business comes to market, a little corner of the landscape shifts. And they're coming at the rate of seventeen new companies every hour.

What banker Nancy Peretsman said was profound and bears repeating: "The great thing about more and more women building and running businesses is that over time the more attractive part of what you see of behavioral elements may make the whole business community swing to that norm. The great thing is that women change the norm."

The big question that now faces women is: Will we change the norm, or will it change us? We've spent a lot of time learning. Perhaps the time has come to teach. So I hope that Nancy is right, that we do change the norm. In a world where most teens don't want to go into business because it is perceived as greedy, where the vast majority of the public distrusts CEOs, and where business is increasingly blamed for most of the world's ills, it is clear that the norm is ripe for change.[1]

So what might the new norm look like? It is one in which executives gain as much respect for nurturing as for toughness. Where quality and output are valued, rather than hours and face time. Where culture, values, and emotional intelligence are part of every corporate score card. The new norm will posit many kinds of entrepreneurs, not just pale young men but men and women of all ages and backgrounds, driven by passion and a desire to serve. And its venture capitalists will considerably expand their mental model of what success looks like.

The new norm is also more outward looking, more flexible than some of the rigid, rules-bound visions of business we've grown up with. I'm struck that the empathy women business owners manifest endows them with a far broader and more holistic vision. They start with other people, and that's what illuminates their market. That is what finds and nurtures their employees. It is what attracts their advisors. It is what keeps their minds supple, alert to signals, sensitive to patterns, and responsive to change. It is other people who keep them going as long as it takes to succeed.

In other words, this new norm operates from a fundamentally different mind-set. It isn't a single, homogenous, uniform mind-set. Quite the opposite. It worships and recognizes the value of diversity. But after watching, meeting, and talking to hundreds of women business owners across industries and geographies, it strikes me that they do share a set of common attitudes, a set of beliefs and imperatives.

Pattern recognition is essential. Broad peripheral vision will keep you better informed than market research.

Intuition, empathy, and a sense of zeitgeist are mission-critical talents. Recognize them, reward them, hone them. People with these talents are much harder to find than number crunchers.

Business isn't rational, and companies are living organisms, not machines. Don't expect them to perform like machines.

A successful company is built on values and a sense of purpose. People want to contribute to something bigger than themselves.

Leadership is orchestration, not command. The true test of leaders may be how little they need to do.

Besides having a market to sell to, culture is the most important thing in business. Nurturing people is the way that companies build value out of nothing.

Great cultures turn personal values into process. It is how cultures survive their founders.

Service is ennobling, not demeaning. Customers are the only source of revenue, and everything else is an expense.

Mistakes are learning. Those who don't make mistakes don't make anything.

Be a good planner but a brilliant improviser. Success hinges on handling surprises, not denying them.

Asking for help is a sign of strength. If you can't accept help, your business will never be smarter than you are.

Families develop professional talents. They aren't competition but sources of education and perspective.

External commitments enhance managerial excellence. All work and no play makes both Jack and Jill stupid and burned out.

To understand the market, you have to spend time in it. Every minute you aren't at your desk, you can be picking up signals.

Emotion is not a weakness. It is inevitable, honest, and an energy source. Recruit people with emotional intelligence who have and inspire passion.

Sustainability is the true hallmark of business success. Profits matter more than revenues.

Stories are us. They're more articulate and more memorable than numbers.

Business is one way of making the world a better place. It is about contributing, not consuming.

Business doesn't follow rules.

These are the beliefs and attitudes that are making women-owned businesses so successful, that are building jobs, revenues, and profits faster than other businesses, that are making women so very successful. They are a good place for *any* business to start.

Can we really do it? Can we really change the business world so much that it comes to respect culture as much as it currently worships technology? Where firing people is *not* a badge of courage? Will women be able to build a business community that values purpose and responsibility at the center of its mission—without being dismissed as weak? Will we ever get large corporations to see that families aren't threatening? Can we really establish sustainability as the ultimate business goal? And can we work together with men to achieve all of this?

We can try. It's a tall order, but we're used to that.

Appendix

OXYGEN MISSION STATEMENT

xygen is on a mission...

To bring you wildly popular entertainment from a woman's point of view.

How do we do it, you ask?

We air relevant and daring programming

...for women and highly-evolved men everywhere.

We honor creativity

...in all things except accounting.

We encourage taking risks

...because the rewards are oh! so much better.

We forge real relationships with employees, audience and partners

...and we always call the day after.

We leverage success

...into lots and lots of success.

And, we have fun doing it

...backwards and in high heels.

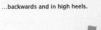

Oxygen is on a mission to bring you wildly popular entertainment from a woman's point of view.

We air relevant and daring programming
...for women and highly-evolved men everywhere.

We honor creativity
...in all things except accounting.

We encourage taking risks
...because the rewards are oh! so much better.

We forge real relationships with our employees, audience and partners
...and we always call the day after.

We leverage success
...into lots and lots of success.

And, we have fun doing it
...backwards and in high heels.

All together now...

EILEEN FISHER MISSION STATEMENT

OUR MISSION

Purpose
To inspire simplicity, creativity, and delight through connection and great design.

Product
To design products that delight the spirit and simplify life.

- To make clothes that work together, guided by these design concepts:

     Simplicity.   Beauty.   Comfort.   Ease.   Versatility.

- To invite every woman to express her own style.
- To produce only what we love.

Practice
To work as a reflection of how our clothing works, simply and in connection.

Profitability
To have our mission drive our business and our profitability foster our mission.

PARTICIPATING COMPANIES

Ambition 24Hours CEO: Penny Streeter	Temporary employment Founded: 1996 Revenues: $110 million Growth Rate: 257 percent Employees: 200+
Andavo Travel Inc. CEO: Brenda Rivers	Travel Founded: 1991 Revenues: $78 million gross Growth Rate: 25 percent Employees: 65; 35 independent contractors
Cenergy Corporation CEO: June Coldren	Oil and gas services Founded: 1998 Revenues: $12 million in 2004 Growth Rate: N/A Employees: 350
Danlee Medical Products Inc. CEO: Joni Walton	Medical supplies Founded: 1994 Revenues: $2.2 million Growth Rate: 64 percent since 1994 Employees: 10

Delaire USA, Inc.
CEO: Lori Hallock
	Telecommunications
	Founded: 1996
	Revenues: 100 percent increase in
	    sales 2004/05, and to double in
	    2006
	Growth rate: 40 percent
	    profitability margin for 2005
	Employees: 16

Edison Automation Inc. COO: Karla Diehl	Automation Acquired: 1999 Growth Rate: 312 percent over 3 years Employees: 70
Eileen Fisher Inc. CEO: Eileen Fisher	Clothing Founded: 1984 Revenues: $190 million Growth Rate: 82 percent over 5 years Employees: 645 (full- and part-time)
Eliassen Group, Inc. CEO: Mona Eliassen	IT Consulting Founded: 1990 Year-on-Year Growth: 30 percent Employees: 500

FlexCorp Systems, LLC
FlexCorp Inc. (California)
CEO: Irene Cohen
	Employment
	Founded: 2001
	Most Recent Annual Revenues:
	  $65 million
	Growth Rate: 700 percent over 5
	  years
	Employees: 100

Frieda's, Inc. CEO: Karen Caplan	Food Employees: 90
ISSI CEO: Cecilia McCloy	Engineering Founded: 1999 Revenues: $7 million Growth Rate: 400 percent over 3 years Employees: 55

Jean's Creams CEO: Jean Soulios	Pharmaceutical Founded: 2003 Growth Rate: 43 percent Employees: 2
Liebler-Bronfman Lubalin CEO: Beth Bronfman	Advertising Founded: 1985 Revenues: $40 million Employees: 12
LopezGarcia Group CEO: Wendy Lopez	Civil engineering Founded: 1988 Revenues: $18.3 million Growth Rate: 18.6 percent Employees: 175

Mavens & Moguls, LLC
CEO: Paige Arnof-Fenn
	Marketing
	Founded: 2002
	Growth Rate: 300 percent each year
	    for 3 years
	Employees: 45 independent
	    contractors

National Van Lines, Inc. CEO: Maureen Beal	Removals Revenues: $91 million Growth Rate: 23.4 percent Employees: 104
Neutral Posture, Inc. CEO: Rebecca Boenigk	Furniture manufacturer Founded: 1988 Revenues: $17 million Employees: 91

NTMI Inc. **(New Technology** **Management Inc.)** CEO: Lurita Doan	Security technology Founded: 1990 Revenues: $210 million in 2004
Open Scan Technologies, **Inc.** CEO: Nadine Lange	Technology Growth Rate: 42 percent Employees: 26
Otis Technology, Inc. CEO: Doreen Marks	Gun-cleaning equipment manufacturer Founded: 1984 Revenue: $15 million Employees: 70
Oxygen Network **Oxygen Media** CEO: Geraldine Laybourne	Cable television Founded: 1990 Growth Rate: 47 percent Employees: 250
SDI CEO: Carmen Castillo	Vendor management Revenue: $150 million Growth Rate: 10 percent Employees: 480
The Pohly Company, Inc. CEO: Diana Pohly	Marketing Acquired: 1996 Growth Rate: 29.6 percent Employees: 52
Thermagon Inc. CEO: Carol Latham	Materials Founded: 1992 Growth Rate: 40 percent Employees: 125

Trade Settlement, Inc. CEO: Pat Loret de Mola	Financial services Founded: 2000 Growth Rate: 100 percent Employees: 8 full-time and 8 full- time independent consultants
WebCT CEO: Carol Vallone	Education technology Founded: 1992 Growth Rate: 50 percent

Notes

Introduction

1. "Access to Capital: Where We've Been, Where We're Going." Center for Women's Business Research, March 2005.

I. The Need to Achieve

1. Women earned 60 percent of all associate's degrees, 58 percent of all bachelor's degrees, and 59 percent of all master's degrees. Data from the National Center for Education, http://nces.ed.gov/fastfacts/display.asp?id=72.
2. Women are "more likely than those who came before them to bring managerial and professional experience to business ownership," according to "Seizing the Opportunities: A Report on the Forces Propelling the Growth of Women-Owned Enterprises," Center for Women's Business Research, June 2003.
3. See Global Entrepreneurship Monitor, www.gemconsortium.org.
4. *Entrepreneurial Vision in Action: Exploring Growth Among Women- and Men-Owned Firms.* The National Foundation for Women Business Owners. February 2001.
5. For more on stereotyping, see Chapter 2 of *The Naked Truth: A Working Woman's Manifesto on Business and What Really Matters,* by Margaret Heffernan, Jossey-Bass, 2004. For boredom, see "Behind the Exodus

of Executive Women: Boredom" by Claudia Deutsch in the *New York Times,* May 1, 2005.

6. Some very interesting work in this area has been done and continues to be done by Alex Haslam at the University of Exeter. In particular, see *The Glass Cliff: Evidence That Women Are Over-Represented in Precarious Leadership Positions* by Michelle K. Ryan and Alex Haslam, *British Journal of Management,* vol. 15, 2004, as well as *The Glass Cliff: Theories That Explain and Sustain the Precariousness of Women's Leadership Positions* by Michelle K. Ryan and Alex Haslam in B. Schyns and J. R. Meindl, *Implicit Leadership Theories: Essays and Explorations,* Information Age Publishing, 2005.

7. *Entrepreneurial Vision in Action,* February 2001.

8. *The Widening Gap: Why American Working Families Are in Jeopardy and What Can Be Done About It* by Jody Heymann, Basic Books, 2000. Quoted in *Seizing the Opportunities,* Center for Women's Business Research, 2003.

9. *Seizing the Opportunities: A Report on the Forces Propelling the Growth of Women* said the desire for more flexibility was the reason they left their position; 23 percent said the glass ceiling blocked their advancement, 23 percent said they were not happy with their job environment, and 21 percent said they were bored or unchallenged.

2. Zeitgeist

1. *Worth the Risk, Women Business Owners and Growth Capital,* Center for Women's Business Research, June 2004.

2. *Working with Emotional Intelligence* by Daniel Goleman. Bantam Books, 1998, p. 33.

3. This is asserted in (among others) *Emotional Intelligence* by Daniel Goleman, Bantam Books, 2005, and also throughout *The Essential Difference* by Simon Baron-Cohen, Basic Books, 2004. Also see *Intuition: Its Powers and Perils* by David G. Myers, Yale University Press, 2004, p. 46, as well as Judith A. Hall, *Nonverbal Sex Differences: Accuracy of Communication and Expressive Style,* Johns Hopkins University Press, 1984.

4. Pink, p. 167.

5. WOW! facts, 2004. See www.ewowfacts.com.

6. *Intuition* by David G. Myers.

7. "Decision Making Styles of Women Business Owners Differs from Male Business Owners," Center for Women's Business Research, June 13, 2006.

8. As well as the NFWBO study cited below, there's an interesting piece of research by Rita Mano-Negrin and Zachary Sheaffer, "Are Women 'Cooler' Than Men During Crises?" It argues that female management styles predispose them to greater strength in crisis management.

9. A 1994 study by the National Foundation for Women Business Owners, "Styles of Succcess: The Thinking and Management Styles of Women and Men Business Owners," shows that women business owners' decision-making style is more "whole-brained" than their male counterparts, and it is more evenly distributed between right brain (intuitive, creative, sensitive) and left brain (logical, analytic, rule-bound) thinking.

3. Niche Is Nice (and Margins Are Marvelous)

1. Seizing the Opportunities: A Report on the Forces Propelling the Growth of Women-Owned Enterprises, Center for Women's Business Research, June 2003. The same report quotes a Venture One report that shows that businesses with a woman CEO received only 69 percent of the $69 million invested in 2000.

2. Global Entrepreneurship Monitor, 2004. www.gemconsortium.org.

3. This is essentially the view of Yankelovich Research, which for years has demonstrated that we now live in a mix-and-match culture.

4. The Value of Values

1. *In Search of Excellence* by Tom Peters and Robert Waterman, Harper & Row, 1982, p. 6.

2. *Authentic Happiness* by Martin E. P. Seligman, Ph.D., Free Press, 2002.

3. See *Bowling Alone* by Robert D. Putnam, Simon & Schuster, 2000.

5. The Power of People

1. *The Enthusiastic Employee: How Companies Profit by Giving Workers What They Want* by David Sirota, Louis A. Mischkind, and Michael Irwin Meltzer, Wharton School Pub., 2005.
2. Ibid.
3. "Troubling Exits at Microsoft," *Business Week,* Sept. 26, 2005. http://www.businessweek.com/@@6Ea0AYUQn6HgVQwA/magazine/content/05_39/b3952001.htm.
4. "Female Bosses Less Likely to Cut Health Benefits" by Jim Hopkins, *USA Today,* Oct. 4, 2005. In firms as a whole during the years 2002 to 2004, the share of employers offering long-term disability insurance dropped from 91 percent to 84 percent.
5. Center for Women's Business Research. Women-owned businesses have workforces that comprise 52 percent women and 48 percent men, whereas men-owned businesses employ 38 percent women and 62 percent men. "Business Owners and Gender Equity in the Workplace," September 2000.
6. WOW! Facts, 2005, p. 40. See www.ewowfacts.com.
7. The trip, however, was not so reliable: When Jamaica Airlines pulled out of Boston, the trip had to be moved to Bermuda.
8. WOW! Facts, 2005, p. 40.

6. Leadership as Orchestration

1. *The Five Dysfunctions of a Team: A Leadership Fable* by Patrick Lencioni, Jossey-Bass, 2002. *Good to Great* by Jim Collins, HarperCollins, 2001.
2. It's an interesting phenomenon of family firms that when taken over by women, they tend to expand and grow at record rates.
3. "Styles of Success: The Thinking and Management Styles of Women and Men Business Owners." Center for Women's Business Research, 1994.
4. *Mavens & Moguls: Because Marketing Matters.* Case study by Myra M. Hart, Kristin J. Lieb, and Victoria W. Winston, Harvard Business School, February 2005.
5. Peter Senge et al., "Looking Ahead: Implications of the Present," *Harvard Business Review,* Sept. 1997.

6. See Appendix for Oxygen mission statement.

7. "More Women at the Top: The Impact of Gender Roles and Leadership Style" by Alice Eagly. Paper presented at *Gender: From Costs to Benefits: 6th Symposium on Gender Research* at Christian-Albrechts University, Kiel, Germany, Nov. 15–17, 2002.

8. Quoted in *Working with Emotional Intelligence* by Daniel Goleman, Bantam Books, 1998, p. 101.

9. James Surowiecki, *The Wisdom of Crowds,* Doubleday, 2004.

7. Customer Love

1. Shoshana Zuboff and James Maxim, *The Support Economy,* Viking, 2002.

2. "Seizing the Opportunities: A Report on the Forces Propelling the Growth of Women-Owned Enterprises," Center for Women's Business Research, 2003.

8. Improvisation

1. *The Essential Difference* by Simon Baron-Cohen, Basic Books, 2004.

2. See "Going Public the Wrong Way" by Emily Barker, *Inc.* magazine, 2002. See also Mary Cantando's *Nine Lives,* Cantando & Associates, 2003.

3. Doris Christopher, *The Pampered Chef,* Doubleday, 2005.

9. Help!

1. "Entrepreneurial Vision in Action: Exploring Growth Among Women- and Men-Owned Firms," Center for Women's Business Research, February 2001.

2. "Excuse Me, May I Have Your Seat?" by Michael Luo, *New York Times,* Sept. 14, 2004. See also *Obedience to Authority: Current Perspectives on the Milgram Paradigm* edited by Thomas Blass. Lawrence Erlbaum Associates, 2000.

3. Women Entrepreneurs Study: A Joint Research Project by Cheskin

Research, Santa Clara University Center for Innovation and Entrepreneurship, and The Center for New Futures, January 2000.

4. Saj-Nicole A. Joni, *The Third Opinion: How Successful Leaders Use Outside Insight to Create Superior Results,* Portfolio, 2004.

5. C200 is a group of high-achieving women who come from the corporate world or from their own businesses. It is restricted to entrepreneurs with revenues of $15 million or more and to corporate women with direct impact on annual revenues of $250 million or more. The WPO is restricted to women owners running product companies with sales in excess of $2 million or service companies with revenues in excess of $1 million. Both organizations have advisory boards themselves.

6. WOW! Facts, 2005, p. 41. See www.ewowfacts.com.

10. Staying Power

1. Daniel Pink, *A Whole New Mind: Moving from the Information Age to the Conceptual Age,* Riverhead Books, 2005.

2. Katherine Ellison, *The Mommy Brain,* Basic Books, 2005.

3. Mary Lou Quinlan, *Time Off for Good Behavior,* Broadway Books, 2005.

4. Marian N. Ruderman and Patricia J. Ohlott, *Standing at the Crossroads: Next Steps for High-Achieving Women.* Center for Creative Leadership, Jossey-Bass, 2002, pp. 115–16.

11. Money Isn't Everything

1. "Gatekeepers of Venture Growth: A Diana Project Report on the Role and Participation of Women in the Venture Capital Industry" by Candida Brush, Nancy Carter, Elizabeth Gatewood, Patricia Greene, and Myra Hart, Kauffman Foundation, 2004.

2. "Not-So-Adventurous Capital," http://www.forbes.com/entrepreneurs/2006/08/30/venturecapital-kleinerperkins-women-cx_mc_0831women.html.

3. "Worth the Risk: Women Business Owners and Growth Capital." Center for Women's Business Research, June 2004.

4. Candida Brush et al., *Clearing the Hurdles: Women Building High-Growth Businesses,* Prentice Hall, 2004.

5. Trish Costello, Center for Venture Education, Kauffman Fellows Program, quoted in "Women Business Owners' Access to Capital."

6. Data from Susan Woodward at SandHill Econometrics.

7. "Access to Capital: Where We've Been, Where We're Going." Center for Women's Business Research, March 2005.

8. Candida Brush, *Clearing the Hurdles,* p. 45. Of the Inc. 500 companies in 2003, 61 percent started with less than $50,000. At the close of 2002, they had aggregate revenues of $14.4 billion, with the median company revenue reported at $10.8 million.

9. "Women Business Owners' Access to Capital."

10. "Women Turn to Other People, Men Go to the Net" by Adam Ritt, in *Better Investing,* March 2005.

11. This quote only from *BusinessWeek,* May 5, 2002. http://www.businessweek.com/smallbiz/0005/ma000502.htm.

12. M & A: Marriage and Acclimatization

1. The multiple causes for M & A failure are extensively and imaginatively reviewed in *Deals from Hell: M & A Lessons That Rise Above the Ashes* by Robert F. Bruner, Wiley Inc., 2005.

13. Birth of a Saleswoman

1. *Entrepreneurial Vision in Action: Exploring Growth Among Women- and Men-Owned Firms.* National Foundation for Women Business Owners, February 2001.

2. *Worth the Risk: Women Business Owners and Growth Capital.* Center for Women's Business Research, June 2004.

3. "When Selling Their Businesses, Women Owners More Likely Than

Men to Care What Happens After the Sale," Center for Business Research, May 2, 2006.

14. The New Norm

1. D. Marlino and F. Wilson, *Teen Girls on Business: Are They Being Empowered?* Committee of 200 and Simmons College of Management, 2002.

   "The Chief Executive," April 2003, http://www.findarticles.com/p/articles/mi_m4070/is_2003_April/ai_99982453.

Bibliography

Bari, Susan Phillips. *Breaking Through: Creating Opportunities for America's Women- and Minority-Owned Businesses,* Women's Business Enterprise National Council, 2004.

Barker, Emily. "Going Public the Wrong Way," *Inc.,* 2002.

Baron–Cohen, Simon. *The Essential Difference: The Truth About the Male and Female Brain,* Basic Books, 2004.

Blass, Thomas. *Obedience to Authority: Current Perspective on the Milgram Paradigm,* Lawrence Erlbaum Associates, 2000.

Bruner, Robert F. *Deals from Hell: M&A Lessons That Rise Above the Ashes,* Wiley, 2005.

Brush, Candida, Nancy M. Carter, Elizabeth Gatewood, Patricia G. Greene, and Myra M. Hart. *Clearing the Hurdles: Women Building High-Growth Businesses,* Prentice Hall, 2004.

Brush, Candida, Nancy M. Carter, Elizabeth Gatewood, Patricia G. Greene, and Myra M. Hart. "Gatekeepers of Venture Growth," a Diana Project Report on the Role and Participation of Women in Venture Capital Industry, Kauffman Foundation, 2004.

Burggraf, Shirley P. *The Feminine Economy and Economic Man,* Perseus, 1999.

Business Week. "Troubling Exits @ Microsoft, *Business Week,* September 26, 2005.

Cantando, Mary. *Nine Lives: Stories of Women Business Owners Landing on Their Feet,* Cantando and Associates, Raleigh, North Carolina, 2003.

Center for Women's Business Research. "Women Business Owners' Access to Capital: Where We've Been, Where We're Going," March 2005.

Center for Women's Business Research. "Worth the Risk: Women Business Owners and Growth Capital," June 2004.

Center for Women's Business Research. "Seizing the Opportunities: A Report on the Forces Propelling the Growth of Women-Owned Enterprises," June 2003.

Center for Women's Business Research. "Entrepreneurial Vision in Action: Exploring Growth Among Women- and Men-Owned Firms," February 2001.

Center for Women's Business Research. "Styles of Success: The Thinking and Management Styles of Women and Men Business Owners," 1994.

Christopher, Doris. *The Pampered Chef: The Story of One of America's Most Beloved Companies,* Currency/Doubleday, 2004.

Collins, Jim. *Good to Great,* HarperCollins, 2001.

Coughlin, Linda, Ellen Wingard, and Keith Holihan. *Enlightened Power: How Women Are Transforming the Practice of Leadership,* Jossey-Bass, 2005.

Deutsch, Claudia. "Behind the Exodus of Executive Women: Boredom." *New York Times,* May 2005.

Diversity Best Practices. WOW! Facts 2005: Women and Diversity, Business Women's Network, 2005.

Diversity Best Practices. WOW! Facts 2004: Women and Diversity, Business Women's Network, 2004.

Donkin, Richard. *Blood, Sweat, and Tears: The Evolution of Work,* Texere, 2001.

Eagly, Alice. "More Women at the Top: The Impact of Gender Roles and Leadership Style." Paper presented at Gender: From Costs to Benefits: 6th Symposium on Gender Research at Christian-Albrechts University of Kiel, Germany, November 15–17, 2002.

Ellison, Katherine. *The Mommy Brain: How Motherhood Makes Us Smarter,* Basic Books, 2005.

Ghoshal, Sumantra, and Christopher Bartlett. *The Individualized Corporation,* HarperCollins, 1997.

Global Entrepreneurship Monitor. 2004, Report

Goleman, Daniel. *Emotional Intelligence: Why It Can Matter More Than IQ,* Bantam Books, 1995.

Goleman, Daniel. *Working with Emotional Intelligence,* Bantam Books, London, 1998.

Gray, Roderick. *How People Work,* Pearson, 2004.

Hall, Judith A. *Nonverbal Sex Differences, Communication, Accuracy and Expressive Style,* Johns Hopkins University Press, 1984.

Hart, Myra M, J. Lieb Kristin, Victoria W. Winston. "Mavens & Moguls: Because Marketing Matters." A case study, Harvard Business School, February 2005.

Haslam, Alex, and Michelle K. Ryan, "The Glass Cliff: Evidence That Women Are Over-Represented in Precarious Leadership Positions," *British Journal of Management,* vol. 15, 2004.

Haslam, Alex, and Michelle K. Ryan. "The Glass Cliff: Theories That Explain and Sustain the Precariousness of Women's Leadership Positions" (see page 10).

Heffernan, Margaret. *The Naked Truth: A Working Woman's Manifesto on Business and What Really Matters,* Jossey-Bass, 2004.

Hopkins, Jim. "Female Bosses Less Likely to Cut Health Benefits," *USA Today,* October 4, 2005.

Joni, Saj-Nicole. *The Third Opinion: How Successful Leaders Use Outside Insight to Create Superior Results,* Portfolio, New York, 2004.

Layard, Richard. *Happiness: Lessons from a New Science,* Penguin Press, 2005.

Lencioni, Patrick. *The Five Dysfunctions of a Team: A Leadership Fable,* Jossey-Bass, 2002.

Mano-Negrin, R., and Z. Sheaffer. "Are Women 'Cooler' Than Men During Crises?," *Women in Management Research,* vol.19, 2004.

Marshall, Paul W., and Julia D. Stevens. "Union Corrugating Company (A) and (B)," Harvard Business School, 2003.

Myers, David G.. *Intuition: Its Powers and Perils,* Yale University Press, 2004.

National Foundation for Women Business Owners. "Entrepreneurial Vision in Action: Exploring Growth Among Women- and Men-Owned Firms," February 2001.

National Foundation for Women Business Owners. "Styles of Success: The Thinking and Management Styles of Women and Men Business Owners," 1994.

O'Reilly III, Charles A., and Jeffrey Pfeffer. *Hidden Value: How Great*

Companies Achieve Extraordinary Results with Ordinary People, Harvard Business Press, 2000.

Persaud, Raj. *The Motivated Mind,* Bantam, 2004.

Peters, Thomas J., and Robert H. Waterman Jr. *In Search of Excellence,* Harper and Row, 1982.

Petzinger, Thomas. *The New Pioneers: The Men and Women Who Are Transforming the Workplace and Marketplace,* Simon & Schuster, 1999.

Pink, Daniel H. *A Whole New Mind: Moving from the Information Age to the Conceptual Age,* Riverhead Books, 2005.

Putnam, Robert D. *Bowling Alone,* Simon & Schuster, 2000.

Quinlan, Mary Lou. *Time Off for Good Behavior,* Broadway Books, 2005.

Ritt, Adam. "Women Turn to Other People, Men Go to the Net," *Better Investing,* published by the Voice of the American Shareholder, March 2005.

Ruderman, Marian N., and Patricia J. Ohlott. *Standing at the Crossroad: Next Steps for High-Achieving Women,* Center for Creative Leadership, Jossey-Bass, 2002.

Seligman, Martin E. P., Ph.D. *Authentic Happiness,* Free Press, 2002.

Senge, P., et al. "Looking Ahead: Implications of the Present," Harvard Business Review, September 1997.

Schyns, B., and J. R. Meindl. *Implicit Leadership Theories: Essays and Explorations,* Information Age Publishing, 2004.

Sirota, David, Louis A. Mischkind, and Michael Irwin Meltzer. *The Enthusiastic Employee: How Companies Profit by Giving Workers What They Want,* Wharton Business School, 2005.

Surowiecki, James. *The Wisdom of Crowds,* Doubleday, 2004.

Taylor, Jim, and Wacker Watts. *The 500-Year Delta,* Harper Business, 1997.

Watson Jr., Thomas J. *A Business and Its Beliefs: The Ideas That Shaped IBM,* McGraw-Hill, 1963.

Wheatley, Margaret J., and Myron Kellner-Rogers. *A Simpler Way,* Berrett-Koehler, 1996.

Women Entrepreneurs Study. A Joint Research Project by Cheskin Research, Santa Clara University, Center for Innovation and Entrepreneurship and The Center for the New Futures. January 2000.

Zuboff, Shoshana, and James Maxmim. *The Support Economy: Why Corporations Are Failing Individuals and the Next Episode of Capitalism,* Viking, 2002.

Acknowledgments

The real heroines of this book are the business owners who have informed it. Some are visible, but many are not. The following provided information, insight, wisdom, and humor for which I am forever grateful: Linda Alepin, Paige Arnoff-Fenn, Ranjit Bajjon, Audrey Baxter, Maureen Beal, Holly Bellingham, Beth Bronfman, Vanessa Buhs, Kimberley Bunting, Karen Caplan, Chris Carosella, Carmen Castillo, Maryann Cataldo, Jane Cavanagh, Candace Chen, Pauline Christie, Irene Cohen, June Coldren, Jacqueline de Baer, Pat Loret de Mola, Karla Diehl, Lurita Doan, Liz Dolan, Risa Edelstein, Di-Ann Eisnor, Mona Eliassen, Rachel Elnaugh, Zena Everett, Marsha Firestone, Eileen Fisher, Nancy Frank, Lynne Franks, Julie Garella, Chey Garland, Jacqueline Gold, Helen Grenier, Adrian Guglielmo, Lori Hallock, Janet Hanson, C. J. Hathaway, Marina Hatsopoulos, Jane Hewland, Diana Hodgkins, Rosie Hunter, Sue Hunter, Liz Jackson, Heather Johnston, Emma Jones, Gloria Ro Kolb, Nadine Lange, Jana La Sorte, Carol Latham, Geraldine Laybourne, Kathy Lehne, Carolyn Leighton, Caroline Liddon, Jane Lighting, Wendy Lopez, Heather Mansfield, Lise Markham, Doreen Marks, Angela Maxwell, Cecilia McCloy, Sylvia Medina, Margaret Milan, Lorna

Moran, Carole Nash, Liz Nelson, Cynthia Nevels, Karen Olson, Nikki Olyai, Diana Pohly, Mary Lou Quinlan, Melodie Reagan, Gail Rebuck, Sharon Reed, Bonnie Reitz, Brenda Rivers, Taryn Rose, Leslie Ross, Karen Sandford, Luisa Scachetti, Dominique Senequier, Laura Sheridan, Donna Shirley, Marcia Shurer, Cindy Solomon, Jean Soulios, Teresa Spangler, Glenda Stone, Penny Streeter, Susan Swan, Joey Tamar, Rose Tempest, Betty Thayer, Eudie Thompson, Jenny Topper, Sarah Tremellen, Lauri Union, Carol Vallone, Joni Walton, Sandra Wear, Cindy Wilson, and Jacqui Withnell.

That women's businesses have made such headway in just a few generations is in itself a fascinating history lesson. Much that has been achieved is due to the efforts of crusading women and mold-breaking research. Without the data to prove the success of women's businesses, we would still suffer from the misconception that all we can run are bed-and-breakfasts and cookie companies. In particular, the Center for Women's Business Research is a model of bulletproof research that changes minds. Juanita Weaver, Moira Lee, and their teams could not have been more helpful. At the National Association of Women Business Owners, Erin Fuller and Amanda Perl were generous in their help and advice. The Women's Business Enterprise National Council, under Susan Phillips Bari, provided priceless insight, experience, and pragmatism to thousands of women's businesses. I'm also grateful to WBENC's Tanya Whiple for sharing her insights so generously. Jill Baker and Julie Weeks at the National Women's Business Council, the Kaufmann Foundation, and the Center for Women's Leadership at Babson College all set a high standard for research, for generosity, and for clear thinking in this area. In addition, the research and thinking that has been done by the following has been illuminating and inspirational: Sharon Begley, Gillian Bowen, Candida Brush, Elissa Ellis, Joyce Fletcher, Rebecca Harding, Brian Headd, Deborah Jacobs, Saj-Nicole Joni, Ilene Lang, Ying Lowrey, Nan Langowitz, Virginia Littlejohn, Rita S. Mano, Deborah Merrill-Sands, Amy Milman, Jan Shubert, Laura Tyson, Fiona Wilson, Linda Tarr-Whelan, Joan Williams, Susan Woodward, and Shoshana Zuboff. It is important, too, to recognize the importance of Tom Peters's evangelism in the cause of women's businesses. As usual, he has been ahead of the curve and unstinting in his support.

Being an entrepreneur can be very lonely, and being a female entrepreneur even more so. But the formidable women's business networks make a huge difference. Their support to me, to their members, and to aspiring entrepreneurs is a model of generosity that anyone would find hard to match. In particular, Marsha Firestone of the Women's Presidents' Organization and Erin Fuller at the National Association of Women Business Owners have proved unstinting in their time, their thoughtfulness, and their wisdom. Springboard, under Amy Milman's expert eye, has helped me with its generosity and insight as it has helped so many women. Similarly, Avivah Wittenberg-Cox at the Professional Women's Network and Glenda Stone at Aurora have been true women's champions. This book could never have been written without them and without the tremendous organizations they run.

Most newspaper, magazine, and business editors seem to feel that women-owned businesses represent a special subject to be looked at occasionally but not as a significant part of the business environment. The editors at Caspian Publishing are the exception. In their coverage of women's businesses and their celebration of women's achievements, Matthew Rock, Stewart Rock, and Adam Leyland have proved unwavering in their commitment and serious attention, and I am indebted to them for their continued support.

Sue Chapman had the unenviable tasks of pulling all the data together and trying to keep up with it. Sue does what women do so well: She pays attention to detail and to people. And it shows. I am immensely grateful to her for outstanding work and incredible patience, often in the face of chaos. I'm also grateful to her husband, Alastair Mearns, for dissecting some of the data that Sue discovered. What mistakes are here are mine; there would have been far more without Sue's vigilance.

Every book is a small business of its own. It has a business plan, it has goals and schedules, it has business partners, and it has its own P&L. The strategic partners for this business have been formidable. There would be no book at all without Clare Alexander and Wendy Wolf. They understood, when many did not, that this was not just a business book, and they showed real passion in supporting it. My editor, Hilary Redmon, has proved that real editors do still exist by making great improvements with grace.

Like companies, all books depend on a dense skein of informal supporters who intervene when they can add value but otherwise stand on the sidelines beaming psychic support. In this regard I will always be grateful to Nick Bicat who was the first person to point out to me just how different men and women are. Rob and Fiona Wilson have (once again) proved themselves true friends and allies, generous in hospitality and encouragement. John Byrne, Guy Edwards, Pam Esty, Gail Evans, Joanne Gordon, Sally Helgesen, Saj-Nicole Joni, Anne Pace, and Pamela Stewart have been wonderful listeners, interrogators, and supporters.

No parent can write a book without support. David Nicholson, Denise Lynn-Nicholson, Rebecca Nicholson, and Liz Edwards have made it possible for me to concentrate without guilt.

Finally, I have to thank my husband, Lindsay, and my children, Felix and Leonora, for putting up with a crazed travel schedule and all the moods that accompany wrestling ideas onto paper. They have taught me how to have a whole life and are my daily reminders that men and women are stronger together than apart. So, no, I didn't write this book just to wind up Dad.

Index